iRPP

Founded in 1972, the Institute for Research on Public Policy is an independent, national, nonprofit organization. Its mission is to improve public policy in Canada by promoting and contributing to a policy process that is more broadly based, informed and effective.

In pursuit of this mission, the IRPP

- identifies significant public policy questions that will confront Canada in the longer term future and undertakes independent research into these questions;

- promotes wide dissemination of key results from its own and other research activities;

- encourages non-partisan discussion and criticism of public policy issues in a manner which elicits broad participation from all sectors and regions of Canadian society and links research with processes of social learning and policy formation.

The IRPP's independence is assured by an endowment fund, to which federal and provincial governments and the private sector have contributed.

Créé en 1972, l'Institut de recherche en politiques publiques est un organisme national et indépendant à but non lucratif.

L'IRPP a pour mission de favoriser le développement de la pensée politique au Canada par son appui et son apport à un processus élargi, plus éclairé et plus efficace d'élaboration et d'expression des politiques publiques.

Dans le cadre de cette mission, l'IRPP a pour mandat :

- d'identifier les questions politiques auxquelles le Canada sera confronté dans l'avenir et d'entreprendre des recherches indépendantes à leur sujet;

- de favoriser une large diffusion des résultats les plus importants de ses propres recherches et de celles des autres sur ces questions;

- de promouvoir une analyse et une discussion objectives des questions politiques de manière à faire participer activement au débat public tous les secteurs de la société canadienne et toutes les régions du pays, et à rattacher la recherche à l'évolution sociale et à l'élaboration de politiques.

L'indépendance de l'IRPP est assurée par les revenus d'un fonds de dotation auquel ont souscrit les gouvernements fédéral et provinciaux, ainsi que le secteur privé.

INSTITUTE FOR RESEARCH ON PUBLIC POLICY

IRPP

INSTITUT DE RECHERCHE EN POLITIQUES PUBLIQUES

Northern Governments in Transition

Political and Constitutional Development in the Yukon,
Nunavut and the Western Northwest Territories

Kirk Cameron & Graham White

Bibliothèque nationale du Québec
Dépôt légal 1995

Canadian Cataloguing in Publication Data

Cameron, Kirk
Northern governments in transition : political and constitutional development
in the Yukon, Nunavut and the Northwest Territories

Includes bibliographical references

ISBN 0-88645-177-9

1. Yukon Territory—Politics and government.
2. Northwest Territories—Politics and government.
3. Nunavut (N.W.T.)—Politics and government.
I. White, Graham, 1948- II. Institute for Research on Public Policy. III. Title.

JL27.5.C35 1995   320.9719   C95-900575-7

Marye Ménard-Bos
Executive Director, IRPP

F. Leslie Seidle
Research Director, Governance Program, IRPP

Copy Editing
Nancy Coté

Editorial Assistant
Chantal Létourneau

Design and Production
Studio Duotone Inc.

Cover Illustration
Studio Duotone Inc.

Published by
The Institute for Research on Public Policy (IRPP)
l'Institut de recherche en politiques publiques
1470 Peel Street, Suite 200
Montreal, Quebec H3A 1T1

Distributed by
Renouf Publishing Co. Ltd.
1294 Algoma Road
Ottawa, Ontario K1B 3W8
Tel.: 613-741-4333
Fax: 613-741-5439

Table of Contents

List of Maps

Foreword

The failure of the Meech Lake and Charlottetown accords has left many Canadians sceptical about Canada's capacity to adapt its Constitution to the realities of the late 20th century. Some, notably in Quebec, see the federal system as a straitjacket that constrains the degree to which the country's regions and communities can realize their particular objectives. Others contend that Canadian federalism is flexible, has evolved considerably since 1867 and will continue to do so. We can expect that debate to continue.

In the meantime, less-noticed but nevertheless significant developments have been taking place in the Canadian North. The most fundamental is the decision to divide the Northwest Territories. In 1999, a new territory, Nunavut, will be established in the central and eastern Arctic. Aboriginal people will have a large majority (more than 80 percent of the residents are Inuit); in this respect, Nunavut will be unique among Canada's constituent units. Already, discussion on implementation suggests certain government structures may also be distinctive. For example, there is serious consideration of an electoral system that would guarantee equal gender representation in the legislative assembly; and the public service will probably be highly decentralized, with departmental head offices located in several communities.

In this book, Kirk Cameron and Graham White recount the events that led to the emergence of Nunavut. Their canvas is much broader, however.

They provide a detailed account of other recent changes in the structure and functioning of government in the Yukon and Northwest Territories, including: the settlement of land claims agreements; the relation between institutions of Aboriginal self-government and public government (i.e., those that apply to all residents); the evolution of the office of Commissioner from, in effect, a colonial-type governor to a post similar to that of a provincial lieutenant governor; and the move toward financing through provincial-type transfers from the federal government. The authors do not advocate provincial status for the territories but include a series of recommendations intended to solidify the devolution that has occurred.

Cameron and White also examine the processes of northern governance, including the non-partisan nature of the present Northwest Territories Legislative Assembly and the strong emphasis on consultation and consensus evident in the Nunavut implementation discussions and the initial steps to develop a constitution for the Western Northwest Territories. The authors draw on extensive consultations with territorial political representatives, public servants and others, and quote extensively from government documents and other primary sources.

Northern Governments in Transition is being published as part of IRPP's Governance project, "Canadian Federalism: Options for Change," which is intended to address fundamental questions about how to structure and govern a country of diverse communities and multiple identities. The previous publications in this series are listed at the back of the book.

As part of its mission, IRPP is committed to encouraging broad participation from all regions and sectors of Canadian society in the discussion and criticism of public policy issues. We are therefore pleased to be associated with this project, which is a timely examination of recent political and constitutional developments in the North. It should be noted, however, that the views expressed here are those of the authors and do not necessarily reflect the opinion of IRPP or its Board of Directors. We hope this study will contribute to the public debate among northern residents that will continue in earnest during the next few years and that many Canadians elsewhere will benefit from the authors' analysis of the changing patterns of governance in our northern territories.

Monique Jérôme-Forget
President, IRPP

Acknowledgements

Many people helped us with this book. Numberless conversations with leaders of Aboriginal organizations, members of the legislative assemblies of the Yukon and the Northwest Territories, journalists, public servants and others have contributed to our understanding of northern governance. A number of people assisted us in more direct ways. We owe special thanks to Peter Russell, who initially suggested our collaboration; thanks also to Doug Bell, John Berg, Alastair Campbell, Frank Fingland, Bernie Funston, Garth Graham, Sheila Meldrum, Daniel P. Odin, John Rayner, Steve Smyth and Liz Snider who read and commented on various drafts; to Gurston Dacks, who tried out early drafts of some chapters on his students at the University of Alberta; to the anonymous referee who made many useful suggestions for improvement; and to Leslie Seidle, Research Director of IRPP's Governance Program, who supported us through the various stages of the project and also offered perceptive criticisms of the manuscript. If errors of fact or interpretation remain, they are the authors' responsibility and in no way reflect the valuable and well-considered advice of those who contributed so generously to the book's preparation.

We gratefully acknowledge the assistance of the Government of the Northwest Territories and of the Government of Canada. Their financial contributions made possible publication of *Northern Governments in Transition*.

Kirk Cameron acknowledges the permission of the Department of Indian Affairs and Northern Development to work on this book; he wishes to make it clear that the views expressed in it are his and do not necessarily reflect those of the Government of Canada.

Finally, our families contributed enormous amounts of support and forbearance. To Nancy, Michael and Andrew Cameron and to Cathy, Kate, Heather and Patrick White our heartfelt thanks.

One

Introduction

It could well be that imaginative political development in the North, with full involvement of the native peoples there, is just the thing we need to remove that nagging doubt whether Canada really is different and really has a character of its own.[1]

Gordon Robertson

Much of our Canadian identity stems from this nation's vast northern expanses. Many Canadians have an emotional, subconscious attachment to the North. This is reflected in widespread interest in the regions which for most Canadians embody the North, the Yukon and the Northwest Territories (NWT). In no part of the country is it difficult to find people who have either lived in or visited one of the territories. Those who have not been to the North often express an interest in travelling there.

Many "southerners" have considerable knowledge of the North. Most Canadians know about the Klondike Gold Rush and are familiar with the search for a Northwest Passage. Robert Service's poems about the North are well known, as are Pierre Berton's writings and Fred Breummer's photographs. Many Canadian homes display Inuit sculpture or paintings by northern artists, such as Ted Harrison, whose inspiration comes either from the northern landscape or from the unique culture and lifestyle of the people of the North.

On a political level, however, Canadians are less well informed. Many are aware that a new territory, Nunavut, is to be established in the eastern and central Arctic in 1999, but few have a clear understanding of just what this will entail. Similarly, few realize that the form and nature of government as they have emerged in the Yukon and the NWT differ substantially from southern Canadian models of governance.

Most Canadians are largely unaware that in the North the fundamental questions about how people will govern themselves are still open, in ways that have not been open in southern Canada for many decades – if indeed they ever were. Fundamental reevaluations are taking place in the territories concerning the orders of government and their interrelationships.

More people live in Prince George, British Columbia or in Sherbrooke, Quebec than in the entire NWT, and the Yukon's population is less than that of either Sydney, Nova Scotia or Belleville, Ontario. Nonetheless, this book is premised on the view that political developments in the northern territories have far greater importance and worth not only to their own people but also to Canada than might be suggested by their populations, and that these developments are worthy of careful analysis and discussion. This view is not solely a land and resource-based argument despite the fact that the NWT and the Yukon comprise nearly 40 percent of Canada's land mass and contain untold natural resources. It is also due to the important and dramatic political and constitutional processes underway in the territories, which are transforming northern society and which have implications and lessons of much wider applicability throughout Canada. After all, the populations of the territories may be small, but their governments face the same range of public policy issues, and they legislate and regulate in most of the same areas as do the provinces. In addition, the territorial governments have the further responsibility of addressing the varying needs and demands of Aboriginal and non-Aboriginal constituencies who approach government from a wide range of cultural, social, economic and political perspectives.

Canadians are increasingly dissatisfied with their governments. Although this is a multifaceted phenomenon, part of the widespread cynicism and disaffection about government is a function of the inability of what are essentially 19th century institutions to cope with 21st century problems. Demands for institutional reform and rethinking of our governmental structures are endemic, and indeed the Institute for Research on Public Policy has identified "governance" as an important focus of attention. In the search for new approaches to governing and new institutional models, the territories offer much food for thought.

It may seem unrealistic romanticism to moot the possibility that governmental innovation in the territories might lead to significant reform in southern Canada where institutions are so much larger and more entrenched. However, in an era which has seen the Berlin Wall fall and communist dictatorships overthrown throughout Eastern Europe, the prospect of political change from unexpected sources ought not to be discounted. On a very practical level, all Canadian governments are grappling with issues of Aboriginal self-government; since Aboriginal people form such a high proportion of the northern population, they could find much of value in the territories' experiences with these questions.

Not only are the forms of government in the territories of interest, but so, too, are the processes by which they are reached. Recent Canadian history has demonstrated that the process of constitutional reform may be as important as its substance. The increasing expectations of people and of organized groups that they will be involved in constitutional change has rendered the process far more complicated and, as a consequence, far more difficult. Again, throughout the North, most particularly in the Western NWT, mechanisms for public involvement in constitutional reform are more extensive than elsewhere in Canada. As former Prime Minister Joe Clark, who chaired the January 1995 Western NWT Constitutional Conference, noted with respect to the inclusiveness and the openness of that exercise: "[It is] highly unusual to bring participants from all communities – this mix of people from leadership to grassroots – together in one place for almost four days of intense discussion in several languages...The courteous, respectful and understanding conduct of [the] deliberations could...be a model for southern Canada and beyond."[2]

After the traumas of the Meech Lake and Charlottetown accords, this country badly needs a constitutional success story. In an important sense, that is precisely what the North can already offer in the creation of Nunavut. Developments in the Yukon and in the Western NWT also hold the potential for dramatic, far-reaching constitutional successes.

These are by no means easy victories, devoid of relevance for larger constitutional processes in Canada. After all, the cultural gulf between Aboriginal and non-Aboriginal peoples of the North is far wider than that between English- and French-speaking Canadians. Moreover, the lack of political homogeneity among the various Aboriginal groups throughout the territories adds to the complexity of the political situation. Similarly, the incompatibility between certain forms of Aboriginal self-government and so-called "public" government in the North makes the problems of integrating a Triple-E Senate into existing national institutions seem straightforward.

Indeed, the common usage of the notion of "public government" in the North is an indication of the distinctive issues of governance there. In most of Canada, the term public government would be redundant; in the Yukon and NWT, however, it is used to denote processes and structures of government applicable to all residents and in which all residents may participate. It is thus distinguishable from Aboriginal self-government, which pertains only to Aboriginal residents, and in which only Aboriginal people participate.

The North offers something of a natural laboratory for the development of government since, in socio-political terms, the Yukon, the Western NWT and the Nunavut region differ markedly from one another. At the same time, complex cultural and lifestyle differences are found within each region.

For instance, the Yukon is home to 14 Aboriginal First Nations that differ in linguistic grouping and in cultural, social and political priorities. Priorities, interests and agendas also vary within the non-Aboriginal community, which makes up four-fifths of the territory's population. Many among this group are passionate defenders of the Yukon as their home. Just as it is wrong to assume that the Aboriginal peoples adhere to a single political agenda or exhibit identical cultures and lifestyles, it is wrong to assume that the non-Aboriginal population is homogeneous. The Yukon is home to a wide range of non-Aboriginal people from white collar civil servants to those whose livelihood is based on hunting and trapping.

The NWT is marked by still greater cultural and social complexities. The 18,000 Inuit who form the majority in the eastern and central Arctic are linguistically and culturally distinct from their neighbours in the territory's northwest, the Inuvialuit. In turn, the Inuit and the Inuvialuit differ very substantially from the Aboriginal population of the Western NWT, the Dene and the Métis. Furthermore, the Dene regional groups, which include the Gwich'in, Sahtu, Dogrib peoples, and the Treaty 8 and Deh Cho First Nations diverge not only in basic political goals but also in the status of their land claims. The Gwich'in and the Sahtu have finalized agreements with the federal government, but the other regional groups are still in various stages of negotiations.

At the same time, the non-Aboriginal people of the Western NWT, an area that will become a separate territory in 1999 when Nunavut comes into existence, represent just over half of the region's population of 34,000.

Despite the common belief that the non-Aboriginal population, largely centred in Yellowknife, is highly transient, increasing numbers of them consider the North their home and are dedicated to building a social and economic community for themselves and their families.

These social complexities will continue to underpin the structure and activities of government in the North. The Yukon and the Northwest Territories are entering a new era in which the government framework[3] has to be built on emerging realities. In the NWT, this includes the division of the territory with the creation of Nunavut, settlement of land claims agreements that have far-reaching direct and indirect effects on government, the interrelationship of public government structures and self-government entities, and continuing provincial-type transfers from the federal government in a time of increasing fiscal constraint. Except for division, the same list applies in the Yukon.

Analysis of government in northern Canada is rendered both more difficult and more interesting by the extraordinary degree to which the political sands continue to shift in such dramatic ways. For example, in November 1994, the Minister of Indian Affairs and Northern Development announced a review of Ottawa's contentious policy of requiring extinguishment of Aboriginal land-based rights as a condition for settling comprehensive land claims. Changing this policy could fundamentally alter the options available to Aboriginal groups that have thus far rejected the comprehensive claim route.

The objectives of this book are threefold. The first is to give the reader an information base regarding the evolution of government in the regions. It will describe how government has evolved in the North, primarily following the Euro-Canadian model of representative and responsible government. Considerable advances have been made in recent years in "patriating" government authority to the territories. The territorial governments are no longer controlled by federal officials. Instead, executives are formed from members of the elected assemblies, which have legislative jurisdictions very similar to those of the provinces; and the executives exercise a range of powers consistent with those of provincial cabinets. Indeed, it could be argued that, as a consequence of the evolution of these forms of government in the North, the territories have taken on a unique constitutional presence in Canada, one which cannot be ignored as the national debate on their status unfolds during the next decades.

The second objective is to assess how the territories are departing from the evolutionary course they had been following until the 1990s.

These departures are in large measure due to the impact of land claims settlements and self-government initiatives on the overall government framework in each of the three regions. Unique approaches are being taken in the North, and the outcome will unquestionably be a blending of the classical government structures found in southern Canada and new arrangements arising from the unique societies and cultures in these regions.

The third objective will be to take the analysis to the national stage and to provide a perspective on how the emerging "new" territories are moving away from the classical provincial government mould. Not only are the three regions different from one another, but they will also ultimately emerge as entities quite different from governments in the south. Because the three territories form an integral part of the national identity, there will be a need for national involvement in the process of confirming the new directions taken in the North.

In short, the book seeks to analyse and to explain the course of political development in the Canadian north, and in doing so to offer territorial political development as a mirror to assist southern Canadians in reflecting upon the future of their own political community.

Notes

1. Gordon Robertson, "Nunavut and the International Arctic," *Northern Perspectives* (Fall 1987), p. 9.

2. Joe Clark, "Concluding Remarks," in Constitutional Development Steering Committee, *Conference Report,* First Constitutional Conference, Western NWT (Yellowknife, 1995), p. 57.

3. The term "government framework" is used in the broadest possible sense and includes the federal government, territorial public government, self-government institutions and administrations, local (municipal) bodies and combined public government/self-government bodies now being established, or planned, in the North.

Two

The Evolution of Government in the Yukon

Introduction

Over the past two or three decades, government in the Yukon has undergone substantial change, evolving from a distinctly limited government very much under Ottawa's direction into a sophisticated "proto-province" with a high level of political autonomy. In comparison to the Northwest Territories (NWT), however, where division and the consequent need to reformulate the Western Arctic's political and governmental structure are fundamentally altering the political landscape, the Yukon exhibits a much more stable social and political environment.

This chapter begins with brief overviews of the Yukon's society and economy and of its political system. The third and fourth sections describe the evolution of the territorial government and its politics. The final section examines the increasingly important relationship between the First Nations and the territorial government from the emergence of Aboriginal people as a political force in the Yukon through the settlement of land claims and self-government agreements with Yukon First Nations.

Society and Economy in the Yukon

Although the Yukon shares obvious and important characteristics with the NWT, the two territories differ substantially in key respects. Most fundamentally, perhaps, whereas Aboriginal people constitute a clear majority in the NWT, they are a minority in the Yukon; they are, in addition, more homogeneous, without the Inuit-Dene-Métis divisions that characterize the NWT. The Yukon is far more urbanized than the NWT and only a small part of it lies north of the treeline. Transportation facilities are far better in the Yukon, and, overall, transportation patterns are quite different within the Yukon and within the NWT.

The population of the Yukon rises and falls with the health of the territorial economy, particularly the mining sector. According to the 1991 census, its population was 27,655,[1] a decline of nearly five percent in the previous few years. (Declining population is hardly a new phenomenon in the Yukon; at the height of the Klondike Gold Rush its population exceeded 50,000, but had declined to 27,000 in 1901 and to barely more than 4000 in 1921.)[2] Some 64 percent of the territorial population – almost 18,000 people – live in Whitehorse, the capital. Watson Lake, near the British Columbia border, Dawson, the former capital, and Faro, the site of a mammoth lead-zinc mine, all have populations of about 1000, but none of the other 15 or so communities has as many as 500 residents.

Except for the community of Old Crow in the far north, all communities are served by an extensive all-weather road system. Whitehorse is, in northern terms, fairly close to Skagway, Alaska, and the Alaska Highway runs from the Yukon into central Alaska. Except in the sparsely populated far north of the territory, where the Dempster Highway leads to Inuvik, the Yukon is separated from the NWT by the formidable Mackenzie Mountains. Accordingly, the Yukon's transportation and communications links tend to be stronger with Alaska and northern British Columbia (and Edmonton) than with the NWT. More than geography is involved in shaping northern transportation and communications patterns; as is often the case with economic hinterlands, links tend to be stronger with the metropolis (in this instance, southern Canada) than between sections of the hinterland.

As in the NWT, government is the largest employer and most important source of economic activity in the Yukon. Mining, followed by tourism, are the next most significant sectors. It is difficult to underestimate the importance of the status of the Faro mine for the economic health of the Yukon, and indeed for the psychic well-being of its population. The mine has closed and re-opened several times in recent years; it has recently been refinanced, and production has resumed. The non-governmental service sector is also important, and some forestry occurs in the southern

Map 1: The Yukon

Source: Department of Indian Affairs and Northern Development, Government of Canada

Yukon. For some Aboriginal people and a few non-Aboriginal people, the subsistence hunting and trapping economy is of major significance.

Approximately 23 percent of the territorial population is Aboriginal; except for some of the very small communities, such as Old Crow and Ross River, the Yukon is predominantly non-Aboriginal. High rates of transiency continue to mark the latter population, though for significant numbers of second- and third-generation non-Aboriginal Yukoners, the territory is their permanent home. Unlike the NWT, the Yukon has no self-identified or organized Métis groups; roughly two-thirds of the Aboriginal population are members of particular First Nations and are therefore beneficiaries under the Yukon land claim.

Government and Politics in Present-Day Yukon

For many years the central political issues for Yukoners were economic development and the desire for greater autonomy from Ottawa; the concerns and wishes of the Aboriginal population on these and other issues were at best of secondary import. Currently, however, the relationship of the Aboriginal and non-Aboriginal populations is the single most important feature of the Yukon political and social landscape. The Macdonald Commission well summarized the fundamental dilemma which underlies so many public policy issues affecting Aboriginal interests in the North:

> The wage economy, particularly that tied to the extraction of non-renewable resources, alienates native people from the land. All aspects of a traditional hunting and gathering society – its social values, political culture, art, legends, religion, social structures – reflect its central purpose of survival through the use of renewable resources. To remove this central purpose and to replace it by either a wage or a welfare economy could destroy the core of native culture and ultimately threaten its survival.[3]

The public policy domain in the Yukon is, however, rendered more complex by the need to balance the Aboriginal agenda with the priorities of other social and economic interests. Many of the non-Aboriginal residents of the Yukon who maintain agendas quite different from those of the Aboriginal peoples are long-term residents, who view themselves not as "outsiders," but as committed Yukoners with an equal stake and investment in its future. This question of balance between Aboriginal and non-Aboriginal interests is a recurring theme of this chapter.

A great many of those who live in the Yukon – Aboriginal and non-Aboriginal – exhibit fierce loyalty and a distinctive pride in the territory, every bit as strong as the loyalties of residents of British Columbia, Quebec and Prince Edward Island toward their provinces.

This strong regional identification is reflected in the political culture of the territory. A central element of the political culture is the vigour and intensity with which Yukoners participate in politics: debates in the Yukon Legislative Assembly are as animated and politically partisan as those in the House of Commons or in provincial assemblies. This intensity and the strong regional loyalty were also evident in the passionate views expressed by both residents and leaders during the national debates on the Meech Lake and Charlottetown constitutional accords. Yukoners of all political stripes vigorously demanded that the territory should not be overlooked in reformulating the constitutional make-up of the nation and that the aspirations of its people should not take second place in political debates over the future of Canada.

A notable sense of permanency surrounds both the definition of the territory and its internal governing structure. In contrast to the experience of the NWT, no changes have occurred to the boundaries of the Yukon since its creation in 1898; nor are any likely to occur in the future. Inhabitants of the Yukon view territorial institutions of governance as permanent, whereas in the NWT a number of Aboriginal groups continue to regard territorial and community government institutions as illegitimate and transitional, to be replaced eventually by more traditional Aboriginal governments introduced through self-government arrangements. The situation in the Yukon reflects in part the numerical predominance of the non-Aboriginal population base.

In addition, however, the Yukon Aboriginal population appears to have accepted the legitimacy of the territorial government. Aboriginal representative political bodies and the territorial government by no means always enjoy harmonious relations, nor do they always agree on the political agenda, let alone on the determination of specific issues. Serious tensions persist between the two constituencies. At the same time, despite such tensions, Yukon First Nations accept the territorial government and work with it to address their political concerns.

What structures of governance have emerged in the Yukon? Notably, as examined later in this chapter, self-government arrangements are being established throughout the Yukon. Nevertheless, in most important respects, "government" in the Yukon continues to be mainly public in nature. As for the form and function of that government, it can perhaps best be understood as a scaled-down version of the provincial governments of southern Canada. The Yukon government is very similar in basic structure – legislature, executive and judiciary – to the standard provincial model. In addition, the operation of its institutions closely follows provincial lines, once allowance is made for its relatively small scale.

The Yukon's Legislative Assembly has 17 members (MLAs), elected in single member constituencies by the familiar "first past the post" electoral system. The assembly's authority derives from what is commonly understood as the Yukon's constitution, the Yukon Act. The list of the Assembly's legislative powers closely resembles the powers exercised by the provinces. Despite having only 17 members, the Assembly's structure and its operating principles are in all essentials the same as those of provincial legislatures. The formal constitutional precepts of the British model of cabinet-parliamentary government are faithfully observed, and the principal political features of Westminster-style parliamentary government are clearly in evidence.

Thus the legislature is dominated by disciplined political parties, the government holds office only so long as it can maintain the confidence of the House, and the style of debate and procedure is highly adversarial and confrontational, reflecting the central government-opposition divide. There is no echo of the "consensus" style of debate and decision making found in the NWT Assembly; instead, as in the south, the Yukon House is marked by high levels of staged and real acrimony between individual members and among parties. Procedurally, the Assembly's operation is highly consistent with the practices in provincial legislatures. The rules of debate and the elements of parliamentary practice (Question Period, readings of bills, clause by clause review in Committee of the Whole and the like), overseen by a neutral Speaker, correspond closely to those of legislatures in southern Canada.[4]

As in the provinces, the territorial executive council – the Cabinet – is comprised of MLAs appointed by the Government Leader (Premier). The current seven-member Cabinet includes five MLAs from the Yukon Party, which assumed power at the 1992 election, and two independent MLAs. Individuals appointed to the executive council are commonly referred to as ministers, and hold portfolios familiar throughout Canada: education, health, human resources, renewable resources, economic development and the like. The constitutional conventions of cabinet solidarity and ministerial responsibility guide executive decision making and, as is the case in southern Canada, the first minister dominates the Cabinet.

In formal terms, under the Yukon Act, the Commissioner is the Chief Executive Officer for the territory. Like provincial lieutenant governors, the Commissioner is appointed for a fixed term by the Government of Canada. Despite the wide-ranging powers the Yukon Act gives to the Commissioner, with few exceptions the latter's role has been reduced to that of a lieutenant governor. The authority that is nominally the Commissioner's under the Yukon Act is in practice exercised by territorial ministers. This is, however, a relatively recent development. As discussed later in this chapter, effective governing authority was transferred from the Commissioner to the elected government in the 1970s and 1980s at the direction of the federal Minister of Indian Affairs and Northern Development who, through section 17 of the Yukon Act, has the authority to restrict the Commissioner's exercise of power.

The executive administers a bureaucratic structure similar to those found in southern Canada. Deputy Ministers serving at pleasure administer departments whose responsibilities and functions relate to the ministers' portfolios. Centralized and hierarchical, the territorial bureaucracy is overwhelmingly dominated by non-Aboriginals, whose management styles and conceptions of bureaucratic practices are very much in accord with those of their southern counterparts. Indeed, as in the NWT, a substantial proportion of middle and senior officials have previously worked in southern governments.

At the judicial level, the court system is similar to those found in the provinces, and includes both territorial courts and the Supreme Court of the Yukon. On a number of occasions during the year territorial court Justices will go on circuit, hearing cases through temporary courts established throughout the Yukon's smaller communities.

Finally, local governments are also based on southern, conventional models. Municipal governments are subordinate entities established through legislation of the territorial government.

Political Development 1870-1960

The territory's political development has tended to reflect economic trends. During prosperous periods such as the Klondike Gold Rush of the 1890s and the expansion of infrastructure during and following World War II, representative and responsible government has been the accepted objective of the evolution of the territorial government. Implicit in this general thrust is the notion that the provincial form, which constituted a foundation of the federation, was the ultimate political goal.

The political dynamics leading to changes in the territorial structures of government throughout this period reflected the thinking and aspirations of non-Aboriginal residents. The Aboriginal people did not figure at all in the debates over such British political values as representative government. Nor were they active participants in territorial politics; the first Aboriginal person was not elected to the Yukon Legislative Assembly until 1978.

Evidence of British political values can be found as early as 1870 in the document that transferred the lands now falling within the Yukon to Canada. This transfer reflected the intention of the Crown and the Government of Canada to set up a province-like territorial regime in the North. Canada's intentions are evident in the address to the Queen that recommended the transfer of Rupert's Land and the North-Western Territories to the Dominion of Canada:

> That the welfare of a sparse and widely-scattered population of British subjects of European origin, already inhabiting these remote and unorganized territories, would be materially enhanced by the formation therein of political institutions bearing analogy, as far as circumstances will admit, to those which exist in the several provinces of this Dominion.[5]

Shortly after the transfer, an amendment to the British North America Act (the Constitution Act, 1871) clarified the Parliament of Canada's power to establish new provinces, although it did not expressly address the creation of new provinces from the territories. The 1871 amendment confirmed that Parliament is responsible for maintaining peace, order and good government in the territories. It also confirmed the creation of Manitoba and gave Canada the capacity to create Saskatchewan and Alberta in 1905.

In 1895, for administrative reasons (largely relating to postal services), the Yukon District was established by Order in Council, followed in 1897 by the creation of the new Yukon Judicial District.[6] The influx of large numbers of prospectors and miners from the United States to the gold fields in the Dawson City area had much to do with these administrative actions.

In 1898, the Yukon Territory was formally created by the Parliament of Canada through the Yukon Act. The language of that statute suggests that the provincial model was the foundation for the structure of government to be established in the new territory. Although an office of lieutenant governor was not created for the new Yukon Territory, as had been the case when the North-West Territories came into being in 1875,[7] an office of Commissioner was established which enjoyed generally the same set of authorities. Section 6 of the Yukon Act, 1898 states that the "Commissioner in Council shall have the same powers to make ordinances for the government of the territory as are at the date of this Act possessed by the Lieutenant-Governor of the North-West Territories."

The act provided for a Council of up to six appointed officials to aid the Commissioner in administering the territory. Within a few years, the local population began to exert pressure for an elected Council. This resulted in a series of revisions to the Yukon Act leading to the transition of the Council from a wholly appointed to a fully elected body, and to an increase in the size of the Council to 10 in 1909.[8] This final step to a fully representative legislature was the last advance in the political development of the territory for the next four decades.

During this period the elected representatives in the territory did not assume any of the executive functions of government. These remained within the purview of the Commissioner, guided extensively by the federal civil service. Federal control would remain until the second half of the century.

The period between 1918 and 1950 has been characterized as the territory's constitutionally "quiet years." Revenues from the gold fields declined steadily after 1910. This was mirrored by the out-migration of "gold-seekers." At the peak of the gold rush, the population was 50,000. The 1921 census reported that it had dropped to 4000.

These trends led Parliament in 1918 to consider legislation abolishing the elected Council. This was perceived by the remaining Yukon non-Aboriginal population as a staggering blow to the British democratic principles that had been so central in the maturation of the territory during the first decade of the century. Pressure from Yukon residents to retain the principle of representative government resulted instead in the reduction of the Council's size to three. As a further cost-cutting measure, the functions of the Commissioner's office and those of the Yukon's Gold Commissioner were amalgamated. An additional cut was made in 1932 with the abolition of the Gold Commissioner and the assumption of the administration of the territory by a Controller.[9]

This would all change as a consequence of World War II. With the threat of Japanese use of the Aleutian Islands as a stepping stone to an invasion of North America, in 1942 Canada and the United States agreed to the construction of the Alaska Highway from northern British Columbia to the interior Alaskan city of Fairbanks. Also in 1942, the Canol Pipeline was also built from Norman Wells in the NWT to a refinery in Whitehorse. Whereas these activities had a positive economic impact for those in the wage economy, for an Aboriginal population that lived primarily off the land, their effects were devastating. During roughly the period of the construction boom, fur prices dropped. In these depressed circumstances many Aboriginal people moved to areas along the new highway system with the hopes of finding employment. Instead of gaining relief from their economic plight, however, the Aboriginal population came into contact with diseases brought in by construction workers; in many cases the consequences were disastrous.[10]

Other road construction activities took place in the 1950s as part of Prime Minister Diefenbaker's Roads to Resources program. This infra-structure development, the "opening" of the territory, has had a permanent impact on the social and economic fabric of the territory, not all positive.

This rapid population, infrastructure and general economic expansion sparked a resumption of activity related to the territory's political status that had been dormant during the "quiet years."

This modern era of territorial political development can be dated from 1948. In that year the office of Commissioner was reestablished. In 1953 a modern day "constitution," the new Yukon Act, was passed by Parliament, giving the Territorial Council a set of legislative powers that in many respects mirrored those exercised by the provinces.

The intentions of the federal government at the time were made clear by the Yukon's Member of Parliament, Aubrey Simmons:

Probably our greatest need today is to encourage new settlers into the northern valleys...Settlers from Great Britain and especially the northern countries of Europe should be encouraged. To fill up our northern valleys, where work and wages are available, is one way of adding also to the defence of this country...The development, settle-ment and opening up of the North will vastly increase our national wealth, and provide work and homes for countless thousands of new Canadians...Vigorous development in the northwest is the road to national security, prosperity and welfare.[11]

The familiar economic theme had a two-fold purpose. The economic potential of the North and its importance to the wealth of Canada was recognized. The importance of northern population increase, not only for tapping into the resource wealth, but also for maintaining sovereignty in the northern expanses, was the second objective.

Tellingly, Simmons' address gave no attention to the indigenous population of the territories. The need for European settlers for the purposes of expansion was a consistent theme in the 1950s. Similar attitudes were reflected throughout the 1957 Final Report of the Royal Commission on Canada's Economic Prospects.[12] A statement prepared for the Royal Commission by the Yukon's Commissioner, Frederick H. Collins, reflects a commonly held attitude of the day with regard to the relationship between the Aboriginal population and economic expansion of the North. He was particularly concerned about the plight of the Aboriginal people due to a sharp decline in the price of the furs that generated most of their income, and was clear about the solution:

To solve the Indian's economic problems and to enable him to become more and more self-supporting, the provision of larger opportunities for wage employment on either a full-time or a part-time basis is essential. Through education and vocational training, and through programs designed to facilitate his entrance into other occupations, the Indian will in future be increasingly encouraged to make his full contribution to the territory's economic progress.[13]

These comments underscore the changing approach of the federal administration toward the North, and specifically the growing priority it assigned to moulding the Aboriginal community to fit the national wage economy.

It was in this general context that the Yukon Act came before Parliament and that a new phase of political development in the territory commenced. This era saw the emergence of both Aboriginal and non-Aboriginal political forces that would alter the nature of the territory's political evolution.

The new act alone did not change the ability of territorial residents to manage their own affairs. This would entail a longer process, which unfolded over the subsequent four decades. The authority given to the Council by the Yukon Act continued to be overshadowed by the federal bureaucracy that held the pen when legislation was drafted. Similarly, the executive powers of the territorial government, including preparation of the territorial budget, were still exercised by the Commissioner with direction from Ottawa and advice from senior federal public servants in the Yukon. This continued direct federal involvement in territorial affairs was in large part due to the territorial government's heavy dependence on Canada for revenue; the only appreciable sources of income under its control were liquor revenues and income tax.

Political Development from 1960 to the Present

The period from 1960 to 1980 is one of the most interesting and turbulent in the political development of the Yukon, marked by numerous battles between the elected Council and the federal government, between the Commissioner and the Council, between the Commissioner and either the federal Minister responsible for the North or senior officials in Ottawa, and among Councillors themselves. A journey through the minutes of Territorial Council proceedings is colourful and entertaining. This period also saw the beginning of what became a strong Aboriginal presence on the territorial political stage (discussed in the next section of this chapter).

Notably absent in the political and constitutional development of the Yukon in this period, or indeed at any time, have been major commissions or studies designed to plot the direction of Yukon government. The Yukon has had no equivalent of the Carrothers or Drury reports – federally commissioned studies – that were so critical in the NWT. Nor has it mounted major constitutional enquiries of its own, such as the NWT's Bourque Commission or its current Constitutional Development Steering Committee. The lack of such political-constitutional reviews may reflect not only a far stronger consensus in the Yukon as to the proper course of constitutional evolution than has ever been present in the NWT but also the numerical preponderance of non-Aboriginal residents.

In 1960 the Yukon Act was amended to allow elected Councillors to be appointed to the territory's Advisory Committee on Finance which the Commissioner was obligated to consult in preparing the territorial budget. Prior to this, the Commissioner and senior officials prepared the annual budgets with no formal mechanism for input from elected members of Council. The sensitivities of the Commissioner and his staff were focussed on the priorities and directions set in Ottawa.

Despite its considerable promise, the Advisory Committee on Finance proved largely ineffective. It failed to give Councillors the direct power they sought to develop policy or to set directions for government. The role played by Councillors and by the Advisory Committee on Finance resembled that of an Official Opposition in a provincial legislature.

Although influence was possible through the Committee, ultimately the government of the day, in this case the Commissioner exercising full executive authority, could move in directions either the Commissioner or Ottawa pleased to take without the concurrence of the elected members.

Thus the elected representatives on Council continued to push for greater independence from Ottawa, seeking not only authority to pass territorial ordinances (acts) but also the capacity to make budget allocations and executive decisions. Between 1966 and 1968 serious conflict developed between the federal and territorial governments. Described by the Commissioner at the time, James Smith, as a "great constitutional crisis,"[14] this conflict highlighted the Council's ineffectiveness. In 1967 Ottawa attempted to increase territorial taxation levels. The Council refused to pass the required bill and tried to amend it. A number of attempts by the Council to persuade the federal Minister to modify the tax were unsuccessful. In essence the Council had no "hammer" to apply in these circumstances.

Ultimately a compromise was worked out, largely due to the determined efforts of Commissioner Smith and the members of the Advisory Committee on Finance. They established procedures for involvement by the committee in the development of budgets, and specifically the introduction of a technical Budget Programming Committee made up of Councillors and officials. As Smith noted in 1980, this episode marked an important milestone in the evolution of responsible government in the Yukon:

[It] was the events of those particular 18 months, starting about early 1967 and culminating in the passage of the budget of the territorial Council in 1968, which put in place the procedures that ultimately wound up in the letter that was signed by Mr. Epp here not too long ago that made the Commissioner's duties subservient to the Leader of the majority group in the Territorial legislature.[15]

In 1970, another critical year in the journey toward responsible government, the Minister of Indian Affairs and Northern Development instructed the Commissioner to establish an Executive Committee composed of the Commissioner, the two Assistant Commissioners and two representatives from the ranks of the Territorial Council. For the first time, elected officials were given portfolio responsibilities in the administration of government and seats in the executive body. Norm Chamberlist, a Councillor representing the riding of Whitehorse East, was given responsibility for the Department of Health, Welfare and Rehabilitation. Hilda Watson, from the riding of Carmacks-Kluane, was given the Education portfolio.

Between 1970 and 1979 the ratio of elected to non-elected members of the Executive Committee increased in accordance with instructions issued by the federal minister. During this same period, party politics was increasingly embraced by the political leadership throughout the territory, and ultimately the three national political parties organized territorial wings in advance of the 1978 territorial election. This election returned 11 Progressive Conservatives, two Liberals, one New Democrat and two independents.

Considerable attention was paid during the 1970s in the Territorial Council and in the Yukon media to the transition of government from what was described in the rhetoric of the day as an Ottawa-run colonial regime to a territorial-based responsible government. Control over the affairs of Yukon residents by bureaucrats in Ottawa was perceived increasingly as repugnant to the democratic values upon which government throughout Canada was based.

On March 7, 1977 the Yukon Council, which by then had come to refer to itself as the "Legislative Assembly" (a standard term in British parliamentary tradition), created the Standing Committee on Constitutional Development. Its mandate was to review the evolution of representative and responsible government in the territory and to recommend further steps for the Yukon's political development. The Committee met throughout 1977 and 1978, and issued three reports that promoted continued progress toward "the attainment of fully responsible government for Yukon," which included expansion of the size of the Legislative Assembly, an increase in the elected representation in the Executive Committee and new instructions from Ottawa restraining the Commissioner's exercise of executive authority. Through the committee's reports, the members also called for a new Yukon Act establishing the eleventh province of Canada.[16]

Although a new province was not created, significant changes did occur between 1977 and 1980, in many respects confirming and strengthening earlier steps toward responsible government. As noted above, the 1978 territorial election was the first based on party politics. In 1979 letters of instruction were issued by consecutive Ministers of Indian Affairs and Northern Development, Hugh Faulkner and Jake Epp, curtailing the executive powers of the Commissioner and confirming the transfer of executive authority to the Yukon's elected representatives.[17]

In particular, what has come to be known as the "Epp letter," an instruction issued to Commissioner Ione Christensen in October of 1979, confirmed and detailed the status of representative and responsible government emerging in the Yukon at that time. Its significance lay in its confirmation that elected MLAs, rather than the Commissioner, should run the territorial government. The Epp letter has been criticized as a master stroke of political opportunism, the main purpose of which was to promote the Progressive Conservatives as the party of economic and political progress in the North. Since responsible government, according to this view, had effectively been achieved under the Liberals, the Epp letter was essentially a public relations exercise rather than a genuine constitutional advance. The accuracy of this interpretation is a matter for debate; what is not at issue is that the Epp letter, by formally recognizing the establishment of responsible government in the Yukon, signifies the culmination of the changes occurring during the previous decade.

As of October 5, 1979, with the issuance of the Epp letter, most of the characteristics of provincial-style government had been instituted in the Yukon. The Commissioner was instructed to remove herself from the daily business of government conducted by cabinet collectively and by individual ministers. The Epp letter gave the Government Leader the opportunity to use the title "Premier" (although at the time he chose not to) and to form the executive body, now to be called "Executive Council" or "Cabinet" in a manner consistent with the terminology used in the provinces. It is noteworthy that in a subsequent (1982) letter of instruction from then Minister John Munro to Commissioner Douglas Bell clarifying the intent of the Epp letter, the office of Commissioner was compared to that of Lieutenant Governor:

> [S]ince the instructions of my predecessor, the Honourable Jake Epp, in 1979 instituted a large measure of responsible government in the Yukon, it follows that in performing your responsibilities in this matter, you should be guided by those parliamentary traditions that govern the role of the Governor General and of Lieutenant Governors in selecting a leader of government.[18]

After the watersheds of the 1970s, the 1980s were marked by consolidation of the quasi-provincial structure of government, most notably in the field of finance. The legislature established a public accounts committee early in the decade, but the most significant change in the 1980s related to the federal government's method of funding the territorial government. The Yukon has always depended heavily on federal financial support; on its own, the territorial government could generate at best a quarter of the funding necessary to provide the level of services enjoyed by its residents.

In 1985, a formula financing agreement was negotiated with Ottawa. This has been of considerable importance to the territory's financial stability. The five-year time frame of the original and subsequent agreements has given the territorial government a better picture of its revenues well into the future, thereby providing a greater capacity for long-term planning. This has been particularly important in a territory dominated by the boom and bust cycles of an economy heavily dependent on mining.

The formula approach also gives the territorial government autonomy to budget according to its own priorities. For instance, before the formula was introduced, a substantial redirection of funding from social services to education to meet the political priorities of the territorial government required federal approval. With the formula in place, the territorial government can redirect funds as it sees fit, which places it in a position of full accountability in balancing the demands of its constituents.

In the late 1980s and early 1990s the administrative picture was dominated by transfers of provincial-type programs from Ottawa to the territorial government. In 1988 the federal government published *A Northern Political and Economic Framework,* which set as an essential policy goal the transfer of "all remaining provincial-type programs to the territorial government, including responsibility for managing the North's natural resources."[19] Inland fisheries, intra-territorial highways, secondary airstrips (known as B and C airports), the Northern Canada Power Commission and a portion of health services, were transferred during this period to add to a wide range of provincial-type programs already delivered by the territorial government. In 1993 negotiations were successfully concluded on a Northern Accord for the management of on-shore oil and gas and revenue sharing for off-shore developments.

Completion of program transfers is viewed by both the federal government and the Yukon as an important step in concluding the evolution of political development in the North. The emphasis on natural resources reflects the importance of reducing the territory's financial dependence on Ottawa. As noted in the *Framework:*

The federal government cannot, nor should it, unilaterally dictate how northern governments evolve. But it can assist this important process by providing a stable and supportive policy framework so that northern governments evolve in a way and at a rate that ensures political stability and sustainable economic growth.[20]

This goal of concluding transfers has yet to be reached owing largely to fiscal limitations and to the unfinished business of settling the remaining First Nations land claims and their self-government corollaries.

The Yukon government has argued that a number of provincial-type programs administered by the federal government are underfunded, and therefore should be "topped up" by the federal government prior to being transferred. Federal transfer guidelines are quite restrictive on this point, but do allow one-time transition costs necessary for transfers to take place.[21]

Most of the pending transfers relate to land and resources, which are also a central focus of the interests of the Yukon Aboriginal people as reflected in negotiations leading to the Yukon land claim. Yukon First Nations believe that further devolution should not interfere with finalization of their claims. Because of the importance of these transfers, the Aboriginal people argue that they should have full party status in the devolution negotiations, including the capacity to veto transfer agreements that are not sensitive to their interests.

Despite this outstanding issue with the Yukon First Nations, there is renewed pressure to step up the pace of transfers. The spectre of future cuts in program spending by Ottawa to control its deficit has added impetus to the territorial government's efforts to take what is available today. For every year that a program remains with Canada under zero budget growth or actual reductions, the territorial government effectively loses ground. This is because the payments made to the territorial government under the formula financing agreement include all transferred amounts and grow annually by a certain factor specified in the agreement. This formula-driven growth, however, does not come into effect until after a transfer has been concluded.[22]

Notably absent from the developments of the 1970s and 1980s has been movement toward provincehood. During the 1979 federal election campaign, Opposition Leader Joe Clark reaffirmed an offer of provincial status for the Yukon that he had made several years earlier. Yukoners, both Aboriginal and non-Aboriginal, were hesitant about pursuing this offer because of uncertainty as to its financial implications and as to how it might affect the resolution of land claims. The Clark government went down to electoral defeat in 1980 before a serious debate could be engaged in the territory.

A decade later, the Penikett government released a green paper on constitutional development in the Yukon which, among other things, raised the issue of provincial status. A select committee of the legislature, established to solicit public reaction, found little interest in constitutional matters generally and only limited support for the idea of the Yukon becoming a province.[23] The attitude of Yukoners toward the territory's constitutional status remains rooted in a practical desire for political autonomy carrying with it the capacity to make important decisions for themselves, particularly those driving the economy, rather than concern with legal formality.

Aboriginal Political Evolution

Any analysis of the Yukon's political development over the past 25 years must take into account the emergence of a strong Aboriginal political presence, which has changed the nature of government in the Yukon substantially. Through the land claim and self-government agreements and in their day-to-day working relations with the Aboriginal community, the federal and territorial governments have come to be integrally tied to the Aboriginal agenda. As political scientist Gurston Dacks has noted, this Aboriginal force is responsible for the Yukon's recent and significant departure from the course of political evolution experienced in the provinces:

> The constitutional development of Canada's northern territories today differs from its historic prairie analogue in that it intimately involves a set of actors who played no direct role in the pursuit of responsible government...the aboriginal peoples of northern Canada.[24]

Federal legislation implementing the Yukon land claim and self-government agreements was passed in June 1994. Passage of the claim bill and the self-government bill marks the culmination of more than two decades of work involving often difficult negotiations among Aboriginal people, Canada and the territorial government. These measures provide the Yukon First Nations with a framework in which permanent relations with the territorial and federal governments will be cemented.

Prior to examining how the Council of Yukon Indians (CYI) claim unfolded, a brief overview of the nature of comprehensive claims is in order. Comprehensive claims such as those in the Yukon and the NWT are, in effect, modern treaties; indeed they are so described in the formal documents. In exchange for financial compensation, fee simple title to certain tracts of land (with ownership of subsurface rights for a small proportion of the land)[25] and participation in wildlife and environmental management boards, the native people extinguish their Aboriginal title to the land covered by the claim (though not other Aboriginal rights). The agreements reached by government and Aboriginal negotiating teams require formal ratification by both sides. For the native people affected this means a referendum, for government it means an act of Parliament. Once confirmed in this manner, the claims achieve constitutional status under section 35 of the Constitution Act, 1982, and may not be altered without the consent of the claimant group.

The money, paid by Ottawa in annual instalments over a period of a decade or more, goes not to individual natives but to designated Aboriginal organizations for economic development projects, social programs and the like. Similarly, the lands retained by the native peoples are held in common by the Aboriginal organization. Specific lands are selected, subject to federal government approval, on the advice of local communities, with a view to ensuring Aboriginal control over important hunting and trapping areas, spiritually significant locales and ecologically sensitive or economically promising potential development sites.

Only a small area in the extreme south-east of the Yukon was ever included under the original treaties covering western and northern Canada. A small number of reserves were established under the Indian Act, but they were primarily intended as hunting and trapping preserves, and no Aboriginal communities have been established on them.

The year 1972 marks the "awakening" of the Aboriginal political movement. In that year a petition was submitted to Parliament by the Aboriginal people of northern Yukon concerning the damage that they considered oil and gas exploration was causing in their traditional homelands. The 1973 publication of *Together Today for Our Children Tomorrow*, by Yukon elder Elijah Smith, was another key event contributing to two decades of intense debate and negotiation between the Government of Canada, the Yukon government and the Aboriginal community, represented ultimately by the Council for Yukon Indians.[26]

The process of negotiating a land claim with Canada was long and often frustrating for both Aboriginal and non-Aboriginal residents of the Yukon. In 1976 and 1984 tentative agreements were reached, but both of them ultimately proved unacceptable to the Yukon First Nations and were rejected by the CYI General Assembly.

In its view, the 1976 agreement did not offer sufficient land or economic and social development commitments. In the absence of a settled claim, the period 1976 to 1980 was marked by tensions arising from the emerging Aboriginal political presence and an increase in control in the affairs of the territorial government by elected Yukon representatives, who were overwhelmingly non-Aboriginal. The two clashed, the controversy centring on the acquisition of land. Non-Aboriginal interests were pressing for the government to make Commissioner's (Crown) land available for sale for various development projects, principally mining and oil and gas exploration. The Aboriginal people of the Yukon maintained that land should not be alienated until their claims were satisfied; they were concerned not only for the principle involved, but also, on a practical level, that sale of prime public land might preempt too many specific areas of the territory by the time their claims were settled. To non-Aboriginal residents, economic development and concomitant political evolution could not occur without a land and resource base from which to generate prosperity and growth.

At various times throughout the negotiations either the territorial government or the CYI withdrew, protesting the actions of the other. An agreement-in-principle (AIP) was finally reached in 1984. The claim was conditional on the Yukon Aboriginal people surrendering their Aboriginal rights, which many on principle refused to do. Thus the AIP was rejected. The AIP also fell victim to a national political debate over self-government and a review of the federal land claims policy that led the Yukon Aboriginal people to believe a better deal could be reached if they awaited the outcome of that national review. This episode illustrates how national political processes influence northern political development.

A new approach was taken when talks resumed in 1985. The highly centralized process aimed at concluding a single claim was replaced by a recognition of the varying needs and priorities of the 10 First Nations comprising the Council of Yukon Indians (the number of First Nations is now recognized as 14).[27] Greater emphasis was placed on Aboriginal community awareness and involvement throughout the negotiation process. It was agreed that a general framework, or umbrella agreement, would be worked out to guide individual First Nations negotiations. The intention was to allow for the priorities of particular First Nations to emerge in specific agreements without jeopardizing the foundations of the agreement available to all First Nations. In a similar sense, individual self-government agreements could be negotiated based on a general framework provided in the First Nations land claim final agreements.

In 1989 a new AIP was signed, and in 1991 an Umbrella Final Agreement (UFA) was reached. The initial four First Nations final agreements and self-government agreements have now been concluded, and the framework is in place for negotiations with the remaining 10 First Nations. In overall terms, the CYI claim involves Aboriginal fee simple title to 41,439 square kilometres of land and payments over 15 years of $242.6 million (in 1989 dollars). The exact amount of land (including land both with and without subsurface rights) and the financial compensation involved in specific claims are variable and open to negotiation, depending on the priorities and the situations of specific First Nations.

As discussed in chapter 5, the land claim and self-government agreements have played a pivotal role in changing the constitutional character of the Yukon territory and in setting a new direction for considering the territory's appropriate place in the overall Canadian constitutional setting.

These agreements have "levelled the playing field" for the Yukon's Aboriginal people in that neither governments nor private resource developers can henceforth ignore their confirmed role in the management of the territory's land and resources. When implemented, the agreements will give First Nations an irrevocable role in land and resource management, not only on settlement lands as defined in the claim, but throughout the territory. The public boards, councils and committees that will control the overall management regime will, in most cases, include 50 percent Aboriginal participation.[28] These public bodies include: Surface Rights Board; Yukon Land Use Planning Council, to which the CYI nominates one-third of the members; Yukon Development Assessment Board; Yukon Heritage Resources Board; Water Board (one-third CYI nominees); and Renewable Resources Councils.

The language of the UFA speaks to the importance of land and resources for the Yukon's Aboriginal population, and to the importance of integrating their interests with those of the general population through instruments of public government. For example, chapter 12 outlines the objectives of the development assessment process. In the words of the agreement, this is to provide a process that

> recognizes and enhances, to the extent practicable, the traditional economy of the Yukon Indian People and their special relationship with the wilderness environment; provides for guaranteed participation by Yukon Indian People and utilizes the knowledge and experience of Yukon Indian People in the development assessment

process; protects and promotes the well-being of Yukon Indian People and of their communities and of other Yukon residents and the interests of other Canadians.[29]

As part of an Aboriginal land claim settlement, this land and resources management framework has been recognized as a fundamental interest of the Aboriginal people of the Yukon and an instrument for the expression of their Aboriginal rights as protected through section 35 of the Constitution Act, 1982. This protection is as yet untested in the courts, but it clearly assures Yukon Aboriginal people that neither the federal nor the territorial government can change the land management structure in the Yukon without the full concurrence of Yukon First Nations. As a component of a land claim over which section 35 protections apply, the Aboriginal place in land and resources use management throughout the territory is guaranteed.

This is not, it must be clarified, equivalent to iron-clad provisions for complete First Nations' control over land and resources in the Yukon. Rather, it is a co-management regime in which Aboriginal participation is guaranteed. Some of the co-management components in the claim were among the most contentious during claims negotiations, in part because the federal departments involved were reluctant to relinquish their jurisdiction. Like those established under the claims in Nunavut and the Western NWT, the boards and councils created through the CYI claim are decision-making, not simply advisory bodies. However, their authority is not absolute, for the federal minister responsible for the North retains the ultimate power to overturn board and council decisions, although this power is unlikely to be exercised except in quite unusual circumstances.

In addition to the focus on land and resources, the Umbrella Final Agreement commits the parties (Canada, Yukon and First Nations) to the negotiation of self-government agreements with each First Nation. A "Model Self-Government Agreement" between Ottawa and the Yukon First Nations was finalized in 1991. It sets the overall framework within which individual First Nations can work to develop detailed self-government arrangements; it thus offers flexibility for individual First Nations together with common provisions applicable to all Yukon Aboriginal groups. First Nations may choose to negotiate the take-up of legislative jurisdiction in most areas now falling within the territorial government's authority. The powers of an individual First Nation can, therefore, reflect the priorities of that community. Those First Nations that have finalized self-government agreements through federal legislation no longer have to operate under the Indian Act. Funding for the self-government arrangements comes in transfer payments directly from the federal government.

A significant element of compromise and accommodation is evident in the self-government agreements. For example, the four First Nations that have finalized self-government arrangements agreed not to exercise their right to legislate matters relating to the administration of justice prior to the year 2000, in order to allow the federal government to develop a national Aboriginal justice policy. Similarly, they agreed not to exercise their taxation powers over real property and over their people for three years to allow the federal government to complete its review of Indian taxation policy.

It is notable that the self-government agreements with the initial four Yukon First Nations describe those eligible to benefit through the agreement as "citizens" of the First Nations. As yet it is unclear what the practical consequences of this highly symbolic term may be. Another potentially significant feature of each self-government agreement is its applicability to all citizens of the First Nation, regardless of whether they live in the settlement lands defined for that First Nation or elsewhere in the Yukon. As Steven Smyth has pointed out, "the self-government arrangements negotiated for Yukon First Nations give them powers and privileges akin to those of provinces in many areas, including privileges that have not been extended to territorial governments in Canada."[30] He cites in this regard the Yukon First Nations' capacity to write and to amend their own constitutions, their authority to legislate without fear of a federal veto and the paramountcy of Yukon First Nations law over Yukon law in matters of general application.[31]

Under the current federal policy, self-government arrangements are to be treated separately from the constitutionally protected claims agreements.[32] Despite CYI insistence that constitutional entrenchment under section 35 be afforded to its self-government agreements, the federal government did not alter its position.

With the election of the Chrétien government in October 1993, however, this separate treatment may change. The Liberal party platform upon which the government was elected recognizes Aboriginal peoples' inherent right of self-government. The government is currently undertaking broad-ranging consultations on this inherent right, which may lead to a new policy and possible future constitutional amendment. The Yukon First Nations self-government agreements provide assurances that they will not limit or jeopardize any future rights determined through the inherent right process. By way of illustration, section 3.3 of the self-government agreement with the Champagne and Aishihik First Nations, whose traditional territory is situated near Haines Junction, stipulates "this Agreement shall not affect the ability of the Aboriginal people of the Champagne and Aishihik First Nations to exercise, or benefit from, any existing or future constitutional rights for Aboriginal people that may be applicable to them." It is possible, therefore, that the self-government agreements, which are already a significant step forward for Yukon First Nations, may be further enhanced in status through the national process.

The self-government agreements give First Nations the capacity to influence the territory's government framework to ensure that it best suits their interests. Where existing public government institutions are not adequately meeting Aboriginal needs, for example, jurisdiction can be taken up by a First Nation, and an appropriate kind and level of service instituted. A range of governance options exist, from a modification of a public program to accommodate Aboriginal interests, through delegation of service delivery responsibility from the territorial to the First Nations government, to full assumption of legislative and delivery responsibilities.

Self-government has an additional economic and social development advantage for the Aboriginal people. By acquiring responsibilities to manage programs and services, First Nations members can take on and benefit from associated training and employment opportunities.

The granting of royal assent to the claims and self-government legislation should not be misinterpreted as the final steps in cementing detailed formal relations between Aboriginal First Nations and the territorial government. There remains an arduous journey of continued exploration and negotiation from which will emerge the details of specific institutional and political relationships between the two cultures. The foundation has been put in place, but the structure requires exhaustive and careful work. Moreover, substantial potential for conflict exists between self-government arrangements and public government in the Yukon, both at the level of specific policy choices and in terms of more basic principles of governance.

Far more is involved here than simply a division of labour between the territorial government and individual First Nations; considerations of cost and of scale can be expected to pit quite fundamental principles of governance against one another, both within the territorial government and within First Nations' governments. All governments will wish to maximize their legitimacy and their autonomy by exercising as wide a range of their formal jurisdictional powers as possible. At the same time, the federal government's commitment to fiscal restraint will sharply restrict funding. It may well be true that public services delivered by small governments that are very close to their people will be better suited to local needs and priorities than services provided by the larger, more remote territorial government. Nonetheless, parallel governmental bodies working in the same policy areas will unquestionably be substantially more costly, particularly given the size of the communities involved. Most Yukon First Nations, after all, number only in the hundreds. Providing services to small numbers of people is inherently expensive. Thus financial pressures will incline First Nations governments to sacrifice autonomy – and perhaps legitimacy – by entering into agreements with the territorial government for joint program delivery. Quite simply, neither form of government will have the resources to go its own way. The Yukon government will enjoy a significant advantage in negotiations toward such agreements on account of its size and the economies of scale it represents, but it cannot presume that First Nations will give up their hard-won self-governing power without expecting in return significant enhancements in the territorial government's accommodation and sensitivity to Aboriginal and community concerns. In addition, individual First Nations may prefer to cooperate on program delivery, or at least strike a common negotiating position *vis-à-vis* the territorial government; this would markedly improve their negotiating position.

The Yukon First Nations are coming to recognize that they will lack both the funding and the capacity to mount by themselves the entire range of policies and programs contemplated in their self-government agreements. How this will affect their practical relations with the territorial government remains to be seen. To an important degree, the outcome of these developments will be affected by the nature of the CYI. It is at present highly uncertain whether the strong emphasis in Yukon Aboriginal political culture on individual First Nations will severely limit the CYI's capacity for significant involvement in political and administrative matters or whether it, or its successor, can carve out a meaningful pan-Yukon role in issues of governance.

Emerging New Aboriginal, Non-Aboriginal Relations

Aboriginal involvement in Yukon governance is not only the product of land claim and self-government agreements. A number of important initiatives have also been taken by the Government of Yukon over the past decade that reflect an increasing awareness of the importance of direct Aboriginal involvement in governing institutions and the importance of government to the Aboriginal population.

The Yukon's Human Rights Act, passed in 1987, includes a special reference in its preamble to the important role the Aboriginal people play within the social structure of the territory. It states: "it is just and consistent with Canada's international undertakings to recognize and make special provision for the unique needs and cultural heritage of the Aboriginal peoples of the Yukon."[33]

Between 1984 and 1988 negotiations between Canada and the territorial government led to Canada's recognition of the special status of Aboriginal languages in the Yukon through an Official Languages funding agreement. In 1988 the Yukon passed its Languages Act officially recognizing and protecting the Aboriginal languages.

Significant steps have been taken by the territorial government to increase Aboriginal involvement in education. The 1989 College Act provides for the appointment of three of the 10 members of the Board of Governors from names submitted by Yukon First Nations. The Education Act of 1990 provides similar guarantees of representation and establishes a Central Indian Education Authority. It also compels the Minister of Education to establish courses "respecting the cultural, linguistic, and historical heritage of the Yukon and its Aboriginal people, and the Yukon environment," and to develop "instructional materials for the teaching of Aboriginal languages and the training of Aboriginal language teachers." This level of program-specific detail is unusual in legislation, especially since the minister is given no discretion in these matters; these are mandatory, not permissive sections.

Have these initiatives by the territorial government made any difference? At this early stage, and in advance of the implementation of land claims and self-government arrangements, it is difficult to tell. However, it is significant that progressive steps are being taken outside the claims environment to address the needs of the Aboriginal people who constitute substantially more than just a "special interest" in the territory.

Conclusion

In summary, the Yukon has moved into a new era of its political evolution. A number of factors will significantly influence its development over the next two decades. The new resources boards established by the claim as part of the public government of the Yukon will have a major impact on territorial economic growth, and they will ensure that the Aboriginal community is fully involved in setting these directions. Implementation of self-government agreements in and around established public government institutions and agencies will result in substantial changes to the territorial government. Since the most important of the provincial-type jurisdictions that have not yet been transferred to the Yukon, namely those related to land and resources, carry with them significant revenue components, the conclusion of program devolution from Ottawa to the territorial government will enhance the Yukon's financial autonomy. (Depending on the provisions of the agreement struck with Ottawa and on its willingness to increase tax rates, the territorial government may realize somewhat greater income through this process, the key being that the Yukon government will set tax and royalty rates itself and receive the money directly, rather than through grants from Ottawa.)

Yet a shadow threatens to fall across the territory during this period – a shadow that has already enveloped much of Canada and that the Yukon may not be able to avoid: the state of the national debt and the steps Canada will have to take to control this expanding problem. In the landmark federal budget of February 1995, which slashed funding for some departments by 40 to 50 percent and entirely eliminated a wide range of programs, including such politically sensitive items as the "crow rate" subsidies to western Canadian farmers, spending on Aboriginal and northern matters generally fared relatively well (DIAND's overall funding allocation over a three-year period was increased by more than 10 percent). For the North, however, the picture was less rosy: funding for the Northern Program will decline by about 10 percent over the same period, and, more significantly, Finance Minister Paul Martin put the territorial governments on notice in his budget speech that, like the provinces, they should expect reductions in transfer payments in coming years (he indicated a five percent cut to the expenditure base in 1996-97).[34] It thus remains very much of an open question as to whether the federal government can continue to afford its current levels of financial support to the northern territories.

People in southern Canada tend to presume that the central political-constitutional question for the Yukon is the attainment of provincial status. To be sure, for some Yukoners this is an important goal. Far more important, however, have been the efforts Yukoners have directed at gaining control over their own government. As this chapter has shown, for the non-Aboriginal people of the territory, this goal has largely been achieved. With the finalization of the CYI claim and the signing of self-government agreements, it is also near realization for the Aboriginal people of the

Yukon. The next principal political question in the Yukon will not be so much provincehood as working out the interplay of self-government and public government in the context of uncertain federal financial support.

Notes

1. Unless otherwise indicated, all population and demographic figures are taken or calculated from Statistics Canada, *Canada's Aboriginal Population by Census Subdivisions and Census Metropolitan Areas*, Catalogue 94-326, March 1994, table 1.

2. Figures cited in Patrick Michael, "Yukon: Parliamentary Tradition in a Small Legislature," in Gary Levy and Graham White (eds.), *Provincial and Territorial Legislatures in Canada* (Toronto: University of Toronto Press, 1989), p. 191.

3. Canada, Royal Commission on the Economic Union and Development Prospects for Canada, *Report*, Vol. 3 (Ottawa: Supply and Services Canada, 1985), pp. 351-52.

4. For an overview of the Yukon Assembly, see Michael, "Yukon: Parliamentary Tradition in a Small Legislature."

5. "Order of Her Majesty in Council Admitting Rupert's Land and the North-Western Territory into the Union, At the Court at Windsor, the 23rd day of June 1870," reprinted in H.K. Cameron and G. Gomme, *The Yukon's Constitutional Foundations: A Compendium of Documents Relating to the Constitutional Development of the Yukon Territory*, Vol. 2 (Whitehorse: Northern Directories Limited, 1991), pp. 29-35. There was some question as to whether the 1870 Order transferred the Yukon region, but this was subsequently confirmed by the September 1, 1880 Order in Council. See discussion in B.L. Willis, "The Crown Grant of the Fiat to Sue: Does Her Majesty the Queen in Right of Yukon Exist?", unpublished manuscript, January 1989, p. 14.

6. Cameron and Gomme, *The Yukon's Constitutional Foundations*, Vol. 2, pp. 45-48.

7. Cameron and Gomme, *The Yukon's Constitutional Foundations*, Vol. 2, pp. 36-42 and 50-56. The Yukon formed a part of the North-West Territories until the formal partitioning in 1898 at the creation of the new Yukon Territory, and was governed by the Lieutenant Governor and his Council as provided for through the North-West Territories Act, 1875.

8. For an exhaustive study of the evolution of the Yukon Council from its origins to 1961, see L. Johnson, *History of the First Through Eighteenth Wholly Elective Yukon Councils, 1909-1961*, submitted by the Government of Yukon to the Members' Services Board of the Yukon Legislative Assembly, 1987.

9. For a discussion of the reductions in government spending in the territory for the period 1918 to 1950 see John Donald Hillson, "Constitutional Development of the Yukon Territory, 1960-1970," unpublished MA thesis, University of Saskatchewan, 1973.

10. Among the sources describing the period of expansion during the 1950s and 1960s are Hillson, "Constitutional Development"; Government of Yukon, *From Sisson to Meyer: The Administrative Development of the Yukon Government, 1948-1979* (Whitehorse: Yukon Department of Education, 1987); Michael S. Whittington (ed.), *The North* (Toronto: Royal Commission on the Economic Union and Development Prospects for Canada and University of Toronto Press, 1985); and Gurston Dacks, *A Choice of Futures: Politics in the Canadian North* (Toronto: Methuen, 1981).

11. Canada, House of Commons, *Debates*, October 12, 1951, p. 19.

12. Canada, Royal Commission on Canada's Economic Prospects, *Final Report*, November 1957.

13. F.H. Collins, *The Yukon Territory: A Brief Presented to The Royal Commission on Canada's Economic Prospects*, 1955, p. 10.

14. James Smith, "The Great Constitutional Crisis, 1966-1968," unpublished paper, 1980.

15. Smith, "The Great Constitutional Crisis."

16. Legislative Assembly of Yukon, "First Report of the Standing Committee on Constitutional Development for Yukon," April 20, 1977; "Second Report of the Standing Committee on Constitutional Development for Yukon," December 5, 1977; and "Third Report of the Standing Committee on Constitutional Development for Yukon," 1978.

17. For the text of the Faulkner and Epp letters, see Cameron and Gomme, *The Yukon's Constitutional Foundations*, Vol. 2, chap. 3.

18. Cameron and Gomme, *The Yukon's Constitutional Foundations*, Vol. 2, chap. 3.

19. Indian Affairs and Northern Development Canada, *A Northern Political and Economic Framework*, 1988, p. 5.

20. Indian and Northern Affairs Canada, *A Northern Political and Economic Framework*, p. 5.

21. Cameron and Gomme, *The Yukon's Constitutional Foundations*, Vol. 2, pp. 270-71.

22. For a broad-ranging discussion of the devolution process in Canada's north, see Gurston Dacks (ed.), *Devolution and Constitutional Development in the Canadian North* (Ottawa: Carleton University Press, 1990).

23. Select Committee on Constitutional Development, *Report on the Green Paper on Constitutional Development*, May 1991, pp. 4-6.

24. Gurston Dacks, "Introduction," in Dacks (ed.), *Devolution and Constitutional Development*, p. 1.

25. These lands are expressly stipulated in the agreements not to be "lands reserved for Indians."

26. The CYI was formed in 1973 with the unification of the Yukon Association of Non-Status Indians and the Yukon Native Brotherhood, the latter representing only status Indians.

27. Yukon First Nations are as follows: Carcross/Tagish First Nations; Champagne and Aishihik First Nations; Dawson First Nations; Kluane First Nations; Kwanlin Dun First Nations; Liard First Nations; Little Salmon/Carmacks First Nations; First Nations of Nacho Nyak Dun; Ross River Dena Council; Selkirk First Nations; Ta'an Kwach'an Council; Teslin Tlingit Council; Vuntut Gwitchin First Nations; and White River First Nations.

28. For details on the composition and responsibilities of the public boards, councils and committees relating to resources management see *Umbrella Final Agreement between the Government of Canada, the Council for Yukon Indians and the Government of the Yukon, 1993* (Ottawa: Supply and Services Canada, 1993). This provides the general framework which is reflected in individual First Nations Final Agreements.

29. *Umbrella Final Agreement,* p. 101.

30. Steven Smyth, "The Constitutional Context of Aboriginal and Colonial Government in the Yukon Territory," *Polar Record*, Vol. 29, no. 169 (January 1993), p. 124.

31. Smyth, "Constitutional Context," pp. 124-25.

32. For a recent analysis of the self-government negotiations process in the Yukon and its relationship to the constitution, see Michael S. Whittington, "Aboriginal Self-Government in Canada," in Michael S. Whittington and Glen Williams (eds.), *Canadian Politics in the 1990s*, 4th ed. (Scarborough: Nelson, 1994).

33. Cameron and Gomme, *The Yukon's Constitutional Foundations*, Vol. 2, p. 225.

34. Paul Martin, *Budget Speech*, February 27, 1995, p. 19.

Three

The Northwest Territories: Attempting to Reconcile Public and Aboriginal Self-Government

Introduction

Perhaps the only safe prediction about the future of government in the Northwest Territories (NWT) is that dramatic changes are in store over the next few years. In the most obvious sense, of course, the division of the NWT in 1999 into two new territories will mean a major change in the landscape of governance. More fundamentally, though, the basic structures and processes of government, particularly in the Western Arctic, may look very different from those currently in place.

In this chapter we examine the factors that will come into play as the political situation unfolds in the NWT. The emergence of Nunavut is analyzed in chapter 4. This chapter thus focuses primarily on political and constitutional developments in the Western Arctic.

Following an overview of the political and constitutional issues confronting the NWT, the chapter offers some background by way of a socio-economic profile of the NWT and a brief account of the highlights of political development prior to the 1990s. The following section sketches out the form and operation of the principal institutions of public government in the NWT. In subsequent sections we examine the progress and possible future directions of land claims and of Aboriginal self-government. The final section considers constitutional development in the Western Arctic.

Over the past two or three decades, the central political question to emerge in the NWT has been the relationship of public government (government with authority over and involvement by all residents) to Aboriginal self-government (which applies only to and includes only Aboriginal people). This issue has, of course, also been prominent in the Yukon, but not nearly to the same extent as in the NWT. As discussed later in this chapter, significant elements in the Aboriginal communities envision models of government combining public with Aboriginal self-government. However, many people in the NWT – Aboriginal as well as non-Aboriginal – view the two as fundamentally incompatible. Moreover, most Aboriginal organizations continue to press strongly for self-government regimes that would effectively exclude or bypass the existing public government.

The public/Aboriginal self-government conundrum is complicated by disagreements about the nature and significance of the treaties that cover most of the Western NWT. For many Dene, as expressed in the views of elders, these were peace treaties between sovereign nations that gave up neither ownership of the land nor the Dene's right to govern themselves. Rather, the treaties permitted non-Aboriginal people to use Dene land in return for certain benefits, such as education and health care. The Government of Canada, by contrast, interpreted the treaties as extinguishing Aboriginal title and acknowledging the Dene's acceptance of Canadian government. In Ottawa's eyes these treaties pertain solely to land and economic benefits and involve no provisions as regards governance.

Major regional and tribal differences are evident in the Western NWT in terms of Aboriginal people's willingness to compromise on treaty and claims issues. Dene in the Treaty 8 and in the Deh Cho regions are unwilling to enter into the same sort of land claims negotiations that the Gwich'in and the Sahtu Dene have finalized. They insist instead that all dealings with Canada, whether related to land or to governance, proceed on the basis of the inviolability of the treaties and thus the recognition of extensive Dene prerogatives in matters of governance.

One important corollary of this position is the Aboriginal view of the Government of the Northwest Territories (GNWT). For many years both the federal government and the GNWT were widely and accurately viewed by the native people of the NWT as alien, colonial institutions, which operated with no participation by Aboriginal people and no support from them. The evolution of the GNWT into a government that is highly sensitive to Aboriginal concerns, reflecting the Aboriginal majorities in the Legislative Assembly and in Cabinet, has given Aboriginal people a

Map 2: The Western Northwest Territories

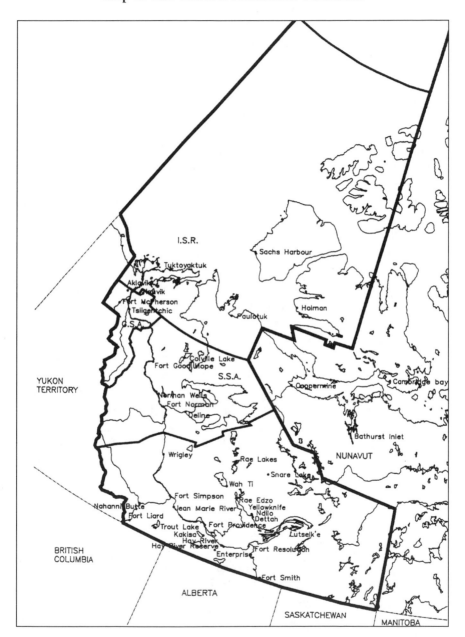

ISR: Inuvialuit Settlement Region GSA: Gwich'in Settlement Area SSA: Sahtu Settlement Area
Source: Constitutional Development Steering Committee, Yellowknife, Northwest Territories

somewhat more favourable view of the territorial government. Although the legitimacy of the GNWT for Aboriginal people varies a good deal from region to region, widespread scepticism remains as to its fundamental nature. The GNWT, particularly its bureaucracy, is still widely perceived as essentially a southern-Canadian style government run along non-Aboriginal lines.

For some Aboriginal organizations, most notably those of the Deh Cho and Treaty 8 regions, rejection of the GNWT is more fundamental still. In their view, since they were not consulted about the creation of the GNWT, let alone asked to approve it, it has no legitimate authority over them. Rather, they believe the treaties confirm that their relationship is directly and exclusively with the Government of Canada. Thus, they maintain that devolution of power from Ottawa to the GNWT is an improper abrogation of Canada's fiduciary responsibilities under the treaties. The federal government, they contend, should be transferring program authority, and the funding to support it, directly to Aboriginal people and not to the GNWT. For similar reasons, they object to Ottawa employing the GNWT as the agent for providing treaty-mandated services, particularly since the federal government funds Indian bands, rather than provincial governments, in southern Canada to deliver many of these services on reserves.

The lack of legitimacy the GNWT enjoys among Aboriginal peoples, the uncertainty about the form and extent of Aboriginal self-government (and, in that context, the role of the federal government) and the inherent instability that characterizes the institutions of public government in the NWT thus render the legitimacy of the GNWT, and its successor in the Western Arctic, highly problematic. The GNWT is clearly a government in transition faced with an extraordinarily complex set of political and constitutional forces.

Society and Economy in the Northwest Territories

The phrase "distinct society" entered the Canadian political vocabulary with the ill-fated Meech Lake Accord's attempt to give constitutional recognition to Quebec's uniqueness. In terms of language, culture, geography and economics, however, the NWT also stands out as the most distinctive society within Canada. Accordingly, before proceeding with the analysis of political and constitutional matters, brief sketches of the societies and economies of Nunavut and of the Western territory seem in order.

Nunavut's population of approximately 21,000 is roughly 83 percent Inuit,[1] distributed across more than two dozen small communities. Iqaluit, with 3500 residents, and Rankin Inlet, with 1700, are the largest communities; another nine have populations of about 1000, and the balance are smaller yet. The non-Aboriginal population is concentrated in Iqaluit (though even there it is a minority) and to a lesser extent in Cambridge Bay and Rankin Inlet; in most communities, the Inuit constitute well over 90 percent of the population. The only communities linked by road are Arctic Bay and nearby Nanisivik; otherwise transportation is by air or water. Virtually all communities have airports or at least air strips, and even remarkably small communities have scheduled air service; fares, however, are high.

The economy of Nunavut is dominated by government and by services. On a territory-wide basis, government at all levels provides over 27 percent of jobs; if government-funded employment in health, social services and education is included, this figure rises to nearly 50 percent.[2] Tourism is an important component in the Nunavut economy. Some mining occurs in the High Arctic, but few of its economic benefits accrue to Nunavut. The potential for additional mining is substantial, but so too are the logistical and economic problems of developing non-renewable resources. Hunting, trapping and fishing do not generate significant amounts of money but are nonetheless important to the economy in providing fresh food (in addition, of course, to their profound cultural significance). In the mid-1980s, the value of "country food" harvested in the NWT was estimated at $40 million annually,[3] and a recent study concluded that "in almost all low income Inuit communities, in-kind income from meat harvests is still more important than employment income; and the combination of meat, fish and fur income is still more important than employment income in most low income Dene communities."[4]

By comparison with the residents of Nunavut, the 36,000 people who inhabit the Western territory live in close proximity and enjoy good communications. However, judged by other standards, the Mackenzie Valley is characterized by substantial distances, sparse population and difficult communications. Nearly half the population, some 15,000 people, lives in Yellowknife, the capital; Fort Smith, Hay River and Inuvik all have populations of roughly 3000; beyond Fort Simpson and Rae-Edzo, the other 22 communities generally have far fewer than 1000 people. A handful of communities are not on the highway system (though several of them are served by ice roads in winter), but this gives a misleading idea of the ease of travel. The Mackenzie Highway ends at Wrigley, leaving a gap of several hundred kilometres to the highways in the Mackenzie Delta (it is possible to drive from communities around Great Slave Lake to Inuvik, but only by a very circuitous route more than 2000 kilometres long through northern British Columbia and the Yukon). Accordingly, as in Nunavut, air travel is extremely important and almost as pervasive.

More politically salient than the geographical distribution of population, though, is its composition. The numbers of Aboriginal and non-Aboriginal residents are effectively equal – according to the 1991 census, Aboriginal people constituted 47 percent of the population. The western territory thus occupies a position between Nunavut where the population is overwhelmingly Inuit, and the Yukon where Aboriginal people are a clear minority. Moreover, the Aboriginal population in the western NWT is not at all homogeneous. The Inuvialuit of the Mackenzie delta and the Beaufort Sea area (who constitute about eight percent of the population) are Inuit, though they do not generally have strong ties to the Inuit of Nunavut and they speak Inuvialuktun, a distinct dialect of Inuktitut, the Inuit language. Approximately 27 percent of the population of the Western territory is Dene, in five separate tribal groupings each with its own language and traditional lands: Chipewyan, Dogrib, South Slave, North Slave and Gwich'in.[5] Finally, some 11 percent of the population are Métis, who are of mixed Dene-white origins.[6] The Métis are an Aboriginal people recognized by the 1982 Constitution Act; in the NWT they are often closely linked to the Dene both culturally and politically. In other ways, however, the Métis differ significantly from the Dene; they are not, for example, "status Indians" under the federal Indian Act. Moreover, the Métis sometimes adopt political positions very different from those of the Dene; Dene-Métis relations vary significantly by region. Certain communities, such as Fort Smith, Inuvik and Aklavik, are marked by considerable diversity of population, but most communities are numerically dominated by single groups. Hay River, Norman Wells and Yellowknife are primarily non-Aboriginal in population (though the capital does contain a substantial – 20 percent – Aboriginal minority); in all other communities, non-Aboriginal residents constitute minorities.

The mainstays of the economy in the western territory are natural resource extraction, government and services. In addition to oil and gas production, the west is (or has been) home to gold, uranium and base metal mines. Extensive exploration in recent years has raised hopes of very substantial diamond mining. One or more major multinational diamond concerns are expected to decide during 1995 whether to proceed with full-fledged mining operations, which could add hundreds of millions of dollars to the territorial economy. Tourism is a significant industry, but apart from arts and crafts, manufacturing is very limited. As in Nunavut, government is by far the largest employer, and service industries such as transportation are also important.

A final note on social conditions. In both Nunavut and the western NWT, Aboriginal people are beset by a host of serious, interrelated social problems: high rates of alcoholism, family violence and youth suicide, pervasive unemployment and welfare dependency, overcrowded housing, lack of education and loss of culture. These social problems are the critical backdrop for constitutional and political reform.

Constitutional and Political Development

Constitutionally and politically, the Northwest Territories has travelled a remarkable distance in a very short time. In the 1950s it was a colonial dependency, administered from Ottawa, delivering only very basic public services. Today the GNWT is a large, sophisticated, democratic government providing a wide range of provincial-type services.

In important respects, the constitutional development of the NWT echoes that of the Yukon. Self-determination came slowly to both territories which, for protracted periods, were directly governed by the federal government. In addition, until the past two or three decades, issues of constitutional development and governance in the two territories were framed and resolved with almost total lack of recognition of the status, needs and values of the Aboriginal peoples. Ironically, the first attempt to divide the NWT in the early 1950s was derailed due to a lack of consultation with northerners, both Aboriginal and non-Aboriginal.

Substantial differences are also evident. As explained in the previous chapter, the Klondike gold rush led to explicit constitutional recognition and a form of self-determination in the Yukon decades before similar developments took place in the NWT. Whereas the Yukon Council and the territorial bureaucracy under the Commissioner (or Gold Commissioner) were always located in the Yukon, such was not the case for the NWT; until the 1960s the NWT Commissioner and the Territorial Council, which passed territorial ordinances (laws), were based in Ottawa. The NWT's greater social diversity and its wider range of political circumstances also required different constitutional and political responses from those that marked the Yukon. At the most elementary level, for example, the Yukon is, in geographic, economic and social terms, relatively homogeneous. By contrast, the most salient characteristic shared by the NWT's diverse regions and peoples is that they constitute the residual left over from the carving out of the provinces and the Yukon from the old North-West Territory.

For the first few decades after 1912, the year the NWT came into being in its present form, government had little presence or significance for most territorial residents. Indeed, the functions of the Ottawa-based civil servants, who ran the NWT, could be better described as administering than as governing. Following the Second World War, Aboriginal people became more closely tied into the wage economy and the mainstream of North American society; greater numbers of non-Aboriginal people came to the NWT to exploit its resources; and the federal government became far more active in providing services such as health, education and housing throughout the North (consistent with the general expansion of the welfare state throughout Canada). The greater responsiveness of the Canadian state to the needs of the Aboriginal people of the North was indeed a mixed blessing, for it came at the cost of government-encouraged migration of Aboriginal people throughout the NWT into permanent communities, with attendant loss of culture and widespread social ills. As with most issues in the North, a simplistic "government wronged the native people" interpretation of these developments overlooks important complexities. If it is true that government officials sometimes favoured relocation for administrative reasons, they nonetheless had a genuine concern for the well-being of the Aboriginal people who, in some cases, were suffering serious hardship from disease, hunger and lack of medical care.

Important policy shifts may have fostered considerable expansion of government operations in the NWT, but the essential nature of government changed little. Beginning in 1951, a few elected members from the Western Arctic joined the Territorial Council, but governing the NWT remained the prerogative of Ottawa's Department of Northern Affairs and Natural Resources. Effective power was principally exercised by the Commissioner, a senior federal civil servant. As Gordon Robertson, who, as Deputy Minister of the Department, held the post of Commissioner from 1953 to 1963, put it, "the Commissioner of that day put Gilbert and Sullivan's Pooh-Bah to shame."[7]

By the mid-1960s, pressure for division of the NWT and a recognition that the basic form of governance required rethinking led to a major review of the way in which government was structured and administered in and for the NWT. In its 1966 report, the Carrothers Commission pro-. posed a series of measures to enhance the autonomy of the GNWT and to increase the degree of political autonomy for the people of the NWT.[8] Its recommendations that Yellowknife become the territorial capital and that the entire apparatus of the territorial administration be transferred to the North were implemented in 1967. Other recommendations, such as the establishment of strong community governments and full "responsible government," took longer to come to fruition or were never fully adopted. The Carrothers Report proceeded from an assumption that government in the NWT would and should be entirely public; in other words, that it should exercise authority over all NWT residents. It did not contemplate any degree of Aboriginal self-government. The Carrothers Commission, according to one recent academic account, "was clearly a white man's commission appointed to investigate the white man's grievances."[9]

Thus, by the early 1970s, the GNWT was headquartered in Yellowknife and was gaining power and responsibility as Ottawa devolved jurisdiction, such as in education and social services. In other, more fundamental ways, however, there was little change. Most notably, the government was not a democratic institution as normally understood in Canada, with executive authority deriving from popular election, and – what amounted to the same thing – Aboriginal people had almost no involvement in it. The Council, which still consisted of both members appointed by the federal government and elected members, could only offer advice to the all-powerful Commissioner, who remained a federal civil servant exercising full executive authority under the NWT Act. The first Aboriginal person was appointed to the Council in 1965, but Aboriginal people remained a minority on the Council and were almost entirely absent from the higher reaches of the GNWT bureaucracy.

In 1974, the federal minister responsible for the North instructed the Commissioner to appoint two elected members of the Council to the Executive Committee, and in the following year the appointment of Council members came to an end. The Council elected in 1975 had for the first time an Aboriginal majority; this continues to the present. The democratically elected Council, however, played only an advisory role to the Commissioner, who effectively continued to control the GNWT.

Of perhaps greater importance for governance in the NWT was the growing militancy and organizational strength of Aboriginal bodies. Politicized by such developments as the federal government's assimilationist white paper of 1969, Ottawa's attempts to create national parks in traditional hunting areas without consulting local communities, and the Berger inquiry into the proposed Mackenzie Valley Pipeline, Aboriginal organizations began to pursue aggressively their goals of political self-determination and control over their traditional lands. The 1975 Dene Declaration calling for "independence and self-determination within the Country of Canada"[10] and the Inuit Tapirisat's 1976 proposal for a separate Inuit homeland represented fundamental challenges to the thrust of political developments in the NWT.

This complex and uncertain situation led the federal government to commission another major review of government in the NWT. The "Drury Report," published early in 1980,[11] took greater account of the perspective of the Aboriginal peoples than did the Carrothers Report, and recommended that resolution of land claims be accorded high priority. However, Drury did not support the idea of dividing the NWT, at least for some time. He stressed the role of community and regional orders of government, in part to give voice to Aboriginal political values and priorities. For all this, the report was premised on a view of public government as pre-eminent. In order to achieve more responsive and democratic government, it recommended a gradual transfer of authority from the Commissioner to the elected council and a cabinet responsible to it. Although this and other Drury recommendations were implemented, many of his key proposals languished; overall, the Drury exercise may have been as important for the ideas and reflections on territorial governance it stimulated as for its specific recommendations.

Public government in the NWT matured to an extraordinary extent during the 1980s. To an important degree, this reflected the willingness of John Parker (who served as Commissioner from 1979 to 1989) to foster representative and responsible government by informally transferring effective governmental authority to elected officials, with the acquiescence of the federal government. Parker gave up chairing (or even attending) the Executive Council, which developed into a traditional cabinet composed entirely of elected members, and he relinquished control over all administrative departments to elected ministers. By the end of the decade, the democratically elected Assembly and cabinet were firmly in control of the GNWT, and the Commissioner's role had become very much akin to that of a provincial Lieutenant Governor.

At the same time, Ottawa continued its policy of devolving provincial-type program authority to the GNWT. The transfer of responsibility for health and of ownership of the NWT Power Corporation to the GWNT during the 1980s resulted in the government exercising a wide range of province-like powers. Ottawa retains jurisdiction in matters of labour law, Crown prosecutions and a few other fields. By far the most important province-like powers yet to be devolved are control over land, more than 90 percent of which remains under direct federal control, and over non-renewable natural resources such as oil and gas and mining. A "Northern Accord" to transfer jurisdiction over oil and gas to the GNWT has been under discussion since the late 1980s. An agreement was almost reached in 1992, but the GNWT held out for a more generous financial settlement than Ottawa was prepared to make (the Yukon did accept a similar offer). Not only are the two governments at odds over the terms of such a transfer, but a powerful coalition of Aboriginal groups has spoken out against it on principle, as it "denies and ignores Dene ownership and interest in the land."[12] Ottawa continues to place high priority on further devolution; a DIAND statement in the wake of the 1995 budget noted that "the federal government will step up efforts to devolve the remaining provincial-type programs to territorial governments."[13]

Consistent with the advances in the Yukon, the basis of federal funding of the GNWT also changed significantly during the 1980s. A complex multi-year, unconditional formula-funding arrangement replaced the annual approval by federal officials for specific program expenditures. This gave the GNWT greater autonomy from the federal government in setting its own spending priorities, although the GNWT remained financially dependent on Ottawa to an extraordinary degree. Indeed, the GNWT continues to receive over 80 percent of its revenue in federal transfers,[14] a far higher proportion than any province (the comparison is slightly misleading, though, since Ottawa receives some minor mining and oil and gas revenues that in the south would accrue to the provinces). As the federal government transferred program responsibilities to the GNWT, it also provided funding for the services, with annual increases built into the formula. At the same time, in acquiring jurisdiction in various policy fields, the GNWT also assumed financial liability for increases in program expenditure (whether from enhanced levels of service or from increases in the costs of program components).

Although Ottawa has treated the territories more generously in recent years than it has the provinces, friction has inevitably developed in federal-territorial finance. For example, the GNWT has claimed that in some instances Ottawa transferred jurisdiction but provided insufficient funding to maintain adequate levels of service. In areas such as social housing and support for Aboriginal languages, territorial officials complain that cuts in federal funding fail to take sufficient account of the NWT's pressing and distinctive needs. One particularly notable dispute was the GNWT's claim that Ottawa owed it nearly $79 million for Aboriginal health care. According to the GNWT, the health transfers of the 1980s did not alter Ottawa's financial responsibility for hospital services the GNWT provided to Inuit and to status Indians throughout the territory. Ottawa maintained that, following the transfers, its responsibilities extended only to costs incurred by Inuit and status Indians at three territorial hospitals and out-of-territory hospitals. The GNWT not only took the matter to court in 1992, but also, citing the large financial burden involved, threatened to return the entire health care system to federal jurisdiction should the dispute not be resolved to its satisfaction.[15] The suit was settled out of court in March 1995, with Ottawa agreeing to a one-time payment of $24 million for claims from 1986-87 to 1991-92. Contribution agreements were also reached under which Ottawa would pay a portion of the GNWT's costs for hospital billings and doctors' services for Inuit and status Indians. The payment was capped at $33.5 million for 1994-95, with annual escalators built in until the agreements expire in 1998 or 1999, when the funding arrangements for Nunavut and the western territory, which will take health costs into account, will come into effect.

Such disputes may involve substantial amounts of money, but they are at root individual, policy-specific quarrels. More fundamental to territorial finance are conflicts over the formula by which Ottawa funds most of the GNWT's operations. Like the provinces, the territories receive federal transfers under Established Programs Financing and the Canada Assistance Plan. Instead of equalization payments, however, the territories receive large unconditional grants according to a complex funding formula that is renegotiated periodically.[16] The GNWT claims that changes Ottawa introduced to the formula in 1989 cost it some $540 million over the period 1990-1995.[17] In the federal budget of February 1995, the territories were notified that in 1996-97 they could expect reductions of five percent in the expenditure base on which formula funding payments are calculated.[18] John Pollard, NWT Finance Minister, estimated that this would cost the GNWT $50 million a year.[19]

The GNWT criticizes in particular the provisions of the formula designed, from the federal perspective, to encourage it to generate more of its own revenue through occupying more tax room (for example, by instituting a territorial sales tax). Thus, what the GNWT terms the formula's "perversity factor" means that as the territory's economy grows and its tax base expands, unless the GNWT levies taxes equivalent to 85 percent of average provincial and local taxation, federal transfers decline. This, in Ottawa's view, simply encourages the GNWT to take reasonable responsibility for financing its own affairs. For its part, the GNWT argues that it represents a disincentive to stimulate economic growth which, under certain circumstances, could result in territorial tax increases producing net losses to the territorial treasury.

The Institutions of Public Government

"Consensus Government"

The institutions of public government in the NWT represent an unusual, indeed unique, blend of traditional British parliamentarianism and northern political culture. Important elements of territorial governance, most notably the operation and style of the Legislative Assembly, demonstrate significant parallels with certain central features of Aboriginal political culture. Yet if the GNWT exhibits an unusual degree of Aboriginal influence, public government in the NWT can hardly be said to operate primarily according to Aboriginal precepts. Instead, it is essentially a southern-style government marked by significant adaptations – some northern, some Aboriginal.

Still, public government in the NWT *is* distinctive and its unique features are important in any consideration of northern government, for they are a measure of northerners' ability to develop methods of governance derived from their own experiences and suited to their own needs.

Perhaps the most distinctive aspect of the GNWT is the absence of political parties in the Legislative Assembly. Most Canadian municipal governments also operate without parties, but the territorial legislature differs fundamentally from them in that it adheres to the principles of British-style "responsible government," essentially as they are practised in the House of Commons and in the provincial legislatures (and in the Yukon Assembly). Thus the territorial cabinet retains office only so long as it maintains the "confidence" of the House; in turn, the Cabinet enjoys a constitutional monopoly over the introduction of spending and taxing measures into the Assembly and a host of formidable executive powers, including control over the territorial public service.

In the NWT, MLAs exercise an unusual degree of policy influence and generally command far more power over the Cabinet than do elected members in southern Canada. To be sure, the Cabinet wields substantially more power than the so-called "ordinary MLAs," but ministers – collectively and individually – are much more accommodating to the suggestions and requests of ordinary MLAs than is the case in the south.

All candidates for territorial office – even ministers seeking re-election – run as independents. After the election, the 24 MLAs gather to select a Speaker, a Premier and the Cabinet. A convention has developed by which four cabinet positions are allocated to the Eastern Arctic and four to the Western Arctic (this is perhaps the most noteworthy illustration of the carefully nurtured political balance between east and west that features prominently in territorial politics). MLAs first elect the Premier, then the balance of the Cabinet by secret ballot.[20] In this way, ministers owe their position in Cabinet to the MLAs rather than to the Premier. These selection procedures are not enshrined in legislation, nor are they set out in the Assembly's rules of procedure, but are practices worked out over time by territorial MLAs. As such, these practices continue to evolve.

The ordinary members have not as yet exercised their power to vote non-confidence in, and thus depose, the entire Cabinet. In the absence of political parties, a more realistic option lies with the MLAs' authority to remove ministers from office, an authority they have exercised on occasion.[21] Since the Cabinet lacks the solid phalanx of party supporters that southern cabinets enjoy, it faces what is, in effect, a permanent 15-8 minority situation (the Speaker only votes to break a tie). Reducing the politics of the Assembly to raw numbers in this way is, however, misleading, not least because it presumes that the dynamic of the Legislative Assembly is primarily one of opposition and confrontation. To be sure, conflict does occur between the Cabinet and ordinary MLAs, but accommodation and cooperation are also common. Conflict also occurs between ordinary MLAs.

Although in both legal and political terms the Cabinet retains final authority, ordinary MLAs are far more deeply involved in the development of government policy than is the case in other Westminster systems. As a matter of course, for example, the Minister of Finance forwards his draft annual expenditure budget to a legislative committee, which reviews it in detail and often makes significant recommendations for change that the government often accepts before finalizing and making public the budget. MLAs also participate in the development of the government's capital budget, which is of such crucial significance to territorial communities and to the stimulation of economic development throughout the NWT.

The authority of the territorial Premier,[22] currently Nellie Cournoyea, is much more constrained than that of southern first ministers. Like the rest of the Cabinet, she is subject to more direct and effective control by MLAs. Moreover, since she does not choose her own ministers, her authority over them is limited. The trend in recent years has been toward enhancing the Premier's power over the Cabinet. In addition to assigning ministers to portfolios, for example, the current Premier received signed, undated letters of resignation from several ministers. Subsequently, she requested and received the resignation of one minister who had apparently lied to the House and another minister accused of improper behaviour. Still, the Premier's ability to discipline or to remove ministers – one of the most formidable powers held by first ministers in Westminster systems – is quite limited and, more generally, so is her capacity to impose her political will upon the Cabinet and legislature.

Two unique structures in the NWT Assembly, caucus and Ordinary Members' Committee (OMC), strongly affect not only patterns of political interaction among MLAs but also public policy. Caucus is a regular, private gathering of all 24 MLAs to discuss political problems. It represents not the formal exercise of power, which remains concentrated in the Cabinet, but a sharing of ideas and information and an attempt to chart directions on important political issues. Caucus meets weekly when the legislature is in session and has recently begun to hold two or three-day strategic planning workshops outside Yellowknife to develop ideas on critical issues such as western constitutional development and the allocation of assets between Nunavut and the western territory.

When the House is sitting, OMC meets every day, in private, to coordinate MLAs' activities and to develop House strategy. Although it is here that MLAs decide whether to "take out" ministers, OMC differs substantially from a southern opposition. It lacks any capacity to discipline its members, and thus often lacks coherence. More significantly, it does not attempt to present either an alternative government or alternative policies. Moreover, its actions (like those of caucus) are more often aimed at resolving problems than at scoring political points or advancing MLAs' political interests.

Two other unusual features of the NWT Assembly warrant attention. First, although almost all debate takes place in English or Inuktitut, the Assembly provides simultaneous interpretation in all of the NWT's eight official languages (Inuktitut, Cree, Dogrib, Chipewyan, Slavey, Gwich'in, English and French). This, as territorial officials point out, is a wider range of simultaneous interpretation than is offered at the United Nations. Secondly, by the standards of the House of Commons and the provincial and Yukon legislatures, the NWT Legislative Assembly conducts its affairs in a remarkably civil way. MLAs listen to one another attentively and do not often interrupt or heckle; even debates on contentious issues proceed in a restrained and orderly fashion.

Politicians in the NWT refer to their system as "consensus government." It is tempting, but probably incorrect, to interpret the territorial legislature as a modern reflection of the traditional Aboriginal style of decision making by consensus. (Not all northern Aboriginal groupings reached decisions through consensus, although this approach to decision making was certainly widespread. It involved extensive, sometimes protracted discussion, in which all participated, and persisted until a clear course of action, acceptable to everyone, emerged. In accordance with the aim of consensus decision making to avoid divisions within the group, votes were not held.) Consensus government, as practised in the territorial legislature, owes more to the absence of political parties than to traditional Aboriginal influences. At the same time, it is no accident that political parties have failed to take hold in the NWT, for they are widely viewed among Aboriginal people as alien, counterproductive institutions, inappropriate for the resolution of northern problems such as land claims, division and self-government.[23]

The resonance with Aboriginal political values, however, probably contributes to the persistence of certain elements of public government in the NWT. The relative civility in the legislature is clearly a function of the distaste in Aboriginal society for confrontation and for interrupting people who are speaking. Similarly, MLAs' unusual degree of influence over policy at least partially reflects the dislike among Aboriginal people for concentrated power. In addition, the lack of Aboriginal enthusiasm for representative (as opposed to direct) democracy is evident in Aboriginal MLAs' preference for serving as the delegates of their communities rather than as trustees exercising personal judgement.

The NWT's unique "consensus government" frequently appeals to southern Canadians alienated by what they see as the mindless partisan bickering and ineffectiveness of their own legislatures. Yet even aside from those in the Aboriginal communities who dispute the GNWT's legitimacy, the people of the NWT are often harshly critical of their system. This negative attitude is a northern variation of the cynicism toward government commonly found throughout North America, heightened by widespread distaste for the behaviour exhibited by MLAs. The record of the 12th Assembly (1991-1995) explains why public perceptions of MLAs are so often unfavourable: of 24 MLAs, one lost his seat upon criminal conviction and another resigned from the legislature after being charged with criminal offenses (the latter had previously resigned from Cabinet when faced with different criminal charges, on which he was acquitted); one minister was forced out of Cabinet for apparently lying to the House; another minister lost her Cabinet seat following her involvement in an alcohol-related altercation in a "dry" community; two ministers were forced out of Cabinet by MLAs dissatisfied with their performances; and the Speaker resigned her position to pursue conflict of interest allegations against a minister, who resigned one of his portfolios but not his Cabinet seat, and in return sued the former Speaker for libel.

The Public Service

Many in the NWT contend that the unusual northern adaptations of the Westminster system are a good deal less significant for territorial governance than the pervasive influence of the southern-style, predominantly non-Aboriginal public service. With a complement of more than 6200,[24] the GNWT is, in territorial terms, a massive organization, and the relatively weak political position of territorial ministers compared to their southern counterparts makes for correspondingly less effective political control over the bureaucracy.

The government that moved from Ottawa to the North in 1967 was firmly based on southern administrative models, and in that sense has changed little since. The GNWT is organized along roughly the same functional lines as provincial public services and has a similar hierarchical structure premised on command and control imperatives. Although the personnel of the GNWT are physically decentralized to an unusual degree – GNWT staff are stationed in all but the smallest communities – effective power remains concentrated in Yellowknife.

A high proportion of senior officials in the GNWT have public service backgrounds in the south. Moreover, the continued reliance on the federal government for program funding through transfer payments imposes certain administrative mechanisms and processes on the GNWT. Despite affirmative action programs, Aboriginal participation in the territorial public service remains low, particularly in senior positions. As of 1992, Aboriginal people constituted approximately 34 percent of territorial public servants but only 14 percent of those in senior management.[25] The territorial Official Languages Act applies to the bureaucracy, and although some progress has been made in the use of Aboriginal languages, most notably Inuktitut, the GNWT remains an overwhelmingly English-language institution. In short, the territorial public service looks much like a scaled-down provincial bureaucracy, and its pervasive influence thus represents an important limit to the distinctiveness of public government institutions in the NWT.

Community and Regional Government

Virtually all official reports and non-governmental studies of governance in the NWT underline the importance of enhancing the powers of community governments, thus echoing the longstanding demands of Aboriginal organizations for more community-centred government. And yet municipal and regional bodies exercise only limited authority in the NWT, principally over such "hard services" as water and sewage. Critical areas of governance, such as economic development and social services are very much centrally controlled, with limited local involvement in setting policy or establishing policy priorities. Regional boards of education and health are partial exceptions, but policy even in these areas is basically directed from Yellowknife. Regional and tribal councils perform advisory rather than policy-making or policy-implementation roles; the limited significance of these bodies is symbolized in the GNWT's acceptance of the Baffin Regional Council's 1992 demise because of financial woes.

Territorial legislation provides for a hierarchy in forms of municipal government, with increasing levels of power and responsibility: settlement, hamlet, village and city. Except for a handful of so-called "tax-based municipalities," local governments have essentially no capacity to generate their own revenue. Thus, their dependence on the GNWT for virtually all their funding is at least as significant in constraining the power of municipalities as their legal status.

Although the official policy of the GNWT for some years has been to strengthen community government, change has been slow. To some extent this reflects concerns in the GNWT bureaucracy (and among some politicians) that small communities simply lack the capacity to administer, let alone develop, all but a limited range of services. Of course, as critics are quick to point out, this rationale coincides with the interest of the public service in maintaining its influence and in avoiding relocation in communities far from the creature comforts of Yellowknife. The GNWT's lack of enthusiasm for strong regional bodies was evident in the Cabinet's rejection of the 1987 report of the Regional and Tribal Councils Review Coordinating Committee, which proposed enhancing the powers of regional and tribal councils.[26] Cynics interpret the GNWT's reluctance to devolve real power to regional bodies as reflecting little more than self-interest (on the premise that regions rather than small, isolated communities, pose the real threat to the entrenched power of the GNWT and its Yellowknife apparatus). The GNWT, however, contends that regional governments would simply be another level of government adding complexity and inefficiency to the system without materially improving services.

The issue of community government is closely linked to questions of Aboriginal self-government. As noted earlier, all but a handful of communities in the NWT are overwhelmingly native in population, though mere numbers are, of course, but one factor in the equation. Aboriginal styles of governance emphasize keeping government close to the people and maximizing popular participation in political decision making. Accordingly, Aboriginal self-government is by its very nature community-centred.

Many communities in the Western Arctic have what amounts to dual government: the municipal council, elected by all residents, and the band council, established under the Indian Act, which deals with certain exclusively Aboriginal matters. Only band members may vote or stand for office in band elections. Since 1988, the territorial Charter Communities Act has permitted communities to establish councils combining the responsibilities of band and municipal councils. Even for matters falling under GNWT jurisdiction, charter community councils possess significantly wider powers than other councils. Until 1993, however, no community had adopted this form of governance; in that year Deline and Tsiigehchic (formerly Fort Franklin and Arctic Red River) became charter communities, and several other communities are exploring this possibility.

Since early 1992, the GNWT has been engaged in a potentially far-reaching realignment of the powers of local government. Through a Community Transfer Initiative (CTI), the GNWT has offered to transfer responsibility to communities for any or all of the programs it delivers. The idea is to devolve jurisdiction rather than simply delegate it or decentralize the operations of the GNWT. Thus communities would be responsible not only for delivering programs but also for developing those programs and for setting policy priorities. Communities are encouraged to put forward proposals (and provided with funds for researching and assembling them) for assuming responsibility either for specific GNWT services or for a wide range of programs. Detailed formal agreements are then negotiated for the transfer of program responsibility, personnel and funding.

Inevitably, perhaps, the CTI has not lived up to its initial promise. Bureaucratic inertia – some would say outright opposition – has taken its toll, and the negotiation process can be protracted and complex. In actual practice, the transfers do not constitute genuine devolution of power to the communities, but involve delegation of the GNWT's program delivery mechanisms. Communities have gained enhanced control over their own affairs through transfers, but their capacity to develop their own programs reflecting their own priorities is restricted by GNWT policies (and by requirements imposed by federal-territorial funding agreements). Moreover, the CTI process has, in several important ways, been overtaken by larger constitutional developments. In the East, the creation of the Nunavut government is a higher priority for many Inuit leaders and communities (though the CTI philosophy mirrors the approach to governance espoused by the Inuit). In the West, since the nature and status of community government is a central question in the constitutional processes currently unfolding, CTI's appeal has diminished and indeed its rationale is not clear. Still, transfers have taken place and others are in train. Most have been limited in scope (for example, an economic development officer), and some communities have not pursued transfers at all. A few communities, however, such as Cape Dorset, have completed extensive transfers covering a wide range of program responsibilities.

Despite its limited success so far, the CTI is important because it opens the way for substantial shifts in governmental authority to local governments. In addition, it also offers at least the potential for melding public government with the principle of greater control by Aboriginal people over their own affairs at the community level.

Land Claims and Self-Government in the Western Arctic

Land claims[27] and Aboriginal self-government share important similarities in that both address native peoples' desires to control their own lives as well as the land and resources so significant to them. A further important similarity has been the central role played by the federal government in both land claims and self-government negotiations. In recent years, the GNWT has taken an increasingly significant part in claims implementation and in self-government negotiations (most of which focus on program areas within territorial jurisdiction). In the NWT, however, as elsewhere in Canada, the claims process has unfolded quite separately from negotiations on self-government. Indeed, whereas three comprehensive land claims have been finalized in the western NWT and a fourth is under negotiation, progress on self-government has been limited. This in part reflects the complex political situation in the west, where the interests and influence of the GNWT, with its extensive program responsibilities, often work against self-government proposals.

It has also been a deliberate policy on the part of the federal government, at least until recently, to keep the claims and self-government processes separate. As a matter of policy, the Conservative government of the 1980s and early 1990s insisted that while the land claims agreements are constitutionally entrenched under section 35 of the Constitution Act, 1982, self-government agreements would not enjoy similar constitutional status.[28] Still, all claims agreements thus far finalized contain provisions alluding to future discussions on self-government, in some cases committing the federal government and the GNWT to self-government negotiations. The Liberal government's explicit acceptance of the premise that Aboriginal people possess the inherent right to self-government signals a major change in policy.[29] The federal government has undertaken extensive consultations to define how this inherent right is to be interpreted and how it is to apply throughout Canada. Accordingly, Aboriginal groups now expect acknowledgement that self-government is constitutionally protected. However, as of early 1995, the federal government had yet to enunciate a clear position on the implementation of the inherent right, and Aboriginal groups throughout the NWT were consequently expressing considerable frustration with the lack of progress on self-government negotiations.

Each comprehensive land claim agreement has unique features, reflecting the priorities of the various Aboriginal groups, the specific context of the individual negotiations and the precedents established in previous claims agreements. At the same time, the three western claims, the Inuvialuit (COPE) claim, the Gwich'in Dene and Métis claim and the Sahtu Dene and Métis claim share important features (many of which are also found in the Inuit claim in the Eastern Arctic). As indicated in the previous chapter, the essential components of northern comprehensive claims are financial compensation, fee simple title to certain tracts of land (with ownership of subsurface rights for a small proportion of the land), and participation in wildlife and environmental management boards in exchange for the native peoples' agreement to extinguish their Aboriginal title to the land included in the claim (though not other Aboriginal rights). As befitting their status as "modern-day treaties," the claims agreements also contain provisions involving the prospect of separately negotiated self-government arrangements.

The planning, wildlife management and other boards created by the claims agreements typically include GNWT nominees and operate in a manner broadly consistent with territorial law. Nonetheless, they clearly have the effect of reducing the scope and authority of the GNWT over important matters of policy and administration.

The Inuvialuit (COPE) Claim

The Inuvialuit of the Mackenzie Delta and Victoria and Banks islands were the first to finalize a comprehensive land claim in the North. Their principal economic and communications ties were with the Western Arctic, and the oil and gas boom in the Beaufort Sea gave particular urgency to the need for Inuvialuit control over their traditional lands. Thus, though they had initially been allied with the Inuit in attempting to create Nunavut, they decided in 1978 to pursue their own claim. Through their political arm, the Committee for Original People's Entitlement (COPE), the Inuvialuit finalized their claim in 1984. The COPE Final Agreement established a series of corporations, such as the Inuvialuit Regional Corporation and the Inuvialuit Development Corporation, to administer the land and the money from the claim and to foster and channel economic development for the benefit of the Inuvialuit. It also provides for several boards – public government boards – through which the Inuvialuit participate in co-management of resources and in environmental protection across the entire settlement area.

Self-government receives only passing mention in the Inuvialuit Final Agreement, but even if the reference is brief, it is nonetheless of great significance. Under the agreement, the federal government guarantees that "the Inuvialuit shall not be treated less favourably than any other native groups or native people [in the Western NWT] with respect to the governmental powers and authority conferred on them."[30] In effect, this provision entitles the Inuvialuit to the equivalent of any self-government arrangement worked out in the Western NWT. To date, the Inuvialuit have favoured strong regional public government over exclusive, ethnically-based Aboriginal self-government in the Mackenzie Delta and the Beaufort area, though they continue to hold the door open to the self-government option should they fail to attain public government institutions suitable to them.[31]

The Gwich'in and Sahtu Claims

Where the Dene and Métis of the western NWT are concerned, the settlement of claims elsewhere in the Western Arctic has proven much more difficult and protracted than it was for the COPE claim. The sometimes differing interests and approaches of the Dene and the Métis, which generated occasional friction and ill feeling, contributed to the complexity of claims negotiations. In addition, the Dene-Métis leadership sought significantly more in their negotiations than had the Inuvialuit. According to a federal account, "they argued forcefully for self-determination in the context of negotiating the land claim."[32] The Dene, for example, set out the following principle in 1976: "Our right to self-government within the Confederation of Canada must be the basis of our new Agreement with the Federal government. Basic to that right is the recognition to exclusive Dene political jurisdiction over the areas of primary importance to our life as a people."[33] Dene-Métis insistence on their treaty rights and the different interpretations of those rights held by Ottawa and by the Dene-Métis further complicated the process.

After difficult negotiations over the better part of two decades, an Agreement-in-Principle (AIP) on a comprehensive claim was reached in 1988 between the federal government and the Dene-Métis of the Western NWT. The AIP and the subsequent Final Agreement held out the prospect of Dene fee simple title to 181,000 square kilometres of land, with subsurface rights to approximately 10,000 square kilometres, and roughly $500 million. Misgivings, particularly among Dene from the Deh Cho and Treaty 8 areas, about extinguishing Aboriginal title to the land and about the lack of self-government provisions in the Final Agreement came to a head in a fractious Dene-Métis joint assembly in July 1990. Representatives of the northern regions, the Gwich'in and the Sahtu, pressed for acceptance. In their view, the Final Agreement, though not ideal, was probably the best that could be attained, and it offered the prospect of political and economic successes like those achieved by the Inuvialuit following settlement of their claim. Dene and Métis from the southern NWT refused to compromise on what they saw as a fundamental issue and pushed to re-open the negotiations. This irreconcilable split effectively marked the demise of the Final Agreement. Ottawa immediately rejected any possibility of renegotiating the agreement but indicated willingness to entertain regional claims modelled on the overall Dene-Métis Final Agreement.

Regionalism – always a strong force in the Western NWT – thus took pride of place over Aboriginal unity, as the Gwich'in and the Sahtu Dene and Métis quickly began claims negotiations. The Gwich'in reached agreement with Ottawa and the GNWT in short order and, with passage of settlement legislation, had a final agreement in place and confirmed by 1992. In the Sahtu, a final agreement was signed in September 1993 and authorized by Parliament in 1994. In the North Slave region, the Dogribs, who found themselves not just geographically but philosophically between the opposing Aboriginal camps, took longer to decide on a course of action. The frenzied diamond rush of the early 1990s, which concentrated on traditional Dogrib lands, and the May 1992 plebiscite on the Nunavut boundary, which the Dogribs saw as encroaching on their territory, were among the factors leading the Dogribs to begin regional claims negotiations in 1993. As discussed below, the Treaty 8 Dene and Deh Cho Dene and Métis have rejected the comprehensive claim route, and are focusing their attention on self-government and on treaty land entitlement processes (though important differences are evident in the approaches and goals of the two regions).

In broad outline, the Gwich'in and Sahtu final agreements resemble the Inuvialuit claim. However, in addition to a host of variations in detail, they also exhibit significant differences (nor are the Gwich'in and Sahtu claims entirely alike). One unusual provision of the Gwich'in claim is its inclusion of hundreds of kilometres of land in the Yukon in the Gwich'in settlement area. Not surprisingly, this provision generated massive political opposition by the Yukon government. Claiming his government had been excluded from the negotiation process, Yukon Premier Tony Penikett objected vehemently to the agreement, which he castigated as showing "profound contempt for the government and the people of the Yukon."[34] (These objections failed to alter the Gwich'in claim, but they did lead to amendments in the CYI claim requiring the approval of the Yukon government for all trans-boundary claims involving the Yukon; this is of particular concern to the Kaska Dena Council in northern British Columbia.)

Under the COPE claim, the interests of the territorial government are recognized, for example in appointments to boards and advisory councils, but generally "government" is taken to mean Canada.[35] The Gwich'in and Sahtu final agreements explicitly define "government" to mean both or either Canada or the GNWT (or its successor),[36] symbolizing the importance of the GNWT in discussions of this nature. More significantly, these two more recent claims include commitments by government to negotiate self-government "appropriate to the unique circumstances of the Gwich'in and in conformity with the Constitution of Canada... [recognizing] the

Gwich'in desire to have self-government exercised as close to the community level as is reasonably possible."[37] Self-government framework agreements are appended to the claims. These framework agreements are short on details but they do stipulate that they aim at "agreements which enable the Gwich'in to govern their affairs and to administer resources, programs and services, as appropriate to the circumstances of the Gwich'in... [and] to describe the nature, character and extent of self-government, the relationship between government and Gwich'in institutions and to accommodate Gwich'in self-government within the framework of public government."[38] This is a pivotal clause, for it signals an expectation that most, if not all, self-government arrangements are to be accommodated within existing, though perhaps significantly modified, territorial and local public government structures. Although the Gwich'in and the Inuvialuit believe they retain the right to develop exclusive Aboriginal self-government institutions in areas such as language, culture and custom adoption, this provision would seem to set an overall direction for self-government negotiations, namely the modification of public government institutions to accommodate Aboriginal representation in decision making and administration. The self-government framework agreements list a wide range of subjects for possible self-government negotiations, including culture and language, housing, taxation, education, social services, health and the administration of justice. In short, they envision potentially far-reaching Aboriginal involvement in governance exercised either through public or Aboriginal self-government structures.

Toward a Constitution for the Western Arctic

With the division of the NWT high on the agenda during the 1980s, it was evident that substantial work would be required to develop a constitutional framework for the new western territory that would emerge from that division. Various proposals were brought forward, and a Western Constitutional Forum (WCF), composed of Aboriginal leaders and MLAs, was established to focus debate and research. In the late 1980s, however, the "Iqaluit Agreement" between the WCF and the Nunavut Constitutional Forum broke down, and the WCF was disbanded as claims settlements became the central political priority in the Western Arctic. Within a few years, though, the Dene-Métis claim had unravelled, replaced by regional claims with self-government provisions, and division by decade's end seemed increasingly likely.

The evident need for a workable constitution for the Western Arctic was matched by widespread unease at the lack of progress on the constitutional front. Early in 1991 an informal "Committee of Political Leaders" – heads of the principal Aboriginal organizations and a few Western MLAs – met in an attempt to renew the western NWT constitutional process. The result was a Commission for Constitutional Development charged with broadly consulting the people and proposing a constitution for public government in the Western Arctic as well as a process for implementing it. The Bourque Commission – named for Jim Bourque, a retired GNWT deputy minister who was also former President of the Métis Association of the NWT – began work in spring 1991 and, after two sets of hearings throughout the Western NWT, reported in April 1992.

Although it recommended that a new western constitution affirm Aboriginal peoples' inherent right to self-government and that, in accordance with Aboriginal interpretations of the treaties, "the spirit, and the meaning and intent of Treaties 8 and 11 be recognized, upheld and protected" in the constitution,[39] the Bourque report did not directly address the relation of self-government to public government. Instead, it proposed vesting most political authority in a "district order of government," which might be public, entirely Aboriginal or some combination of the two. District governments, in this schema, might encompass single communities, such as the City of Yellowknife; regions including a number of communities, such as the Beaufort-Delta region proposed by the Inuvialuit and the Gwich'in; or a single community and its traditional hunting and trapping lands. The central government would exercise only the most restricted powers; in most policy areas, such as education, health and economic development, its role would be limited to setting "standards." A number of mechanisms were discussed to ensure high levels of representation of Aboriginal people and women in the central government.

One of the report's most important principles was the notion that "all authority to govern belongs to the people, collectively, and flows, collectively, from them to their institutions of government."[40] Following this precept, it recommended that its proposals be reviewed and fleshed out in representative constituent assemblies, beginning in fall 1992, and that ratification of a resulting draft constitution be subject to a referendum or plebiscite as well as "consent" – undefined – of Aboriginal peoples.

Response to the Bourque report was, not surprisingly, mixed. For some, it represented a thoughtful and reasonable approach to bridging the chasm between public and self-government; for others, the emphasis

66

on the district order of government portended a balkanization of the Western NWT into inefficient, insular principalities. Yet others believed that the Bourque proposals offered insufficient scope for full Aboriginal self-government. Lack of consensus on substance was compounded by concerns over process. Many non-Aboriginal territorial residents lacked faith that their interests would be accorded the weight their numbers warranted in a process built around constituent assemblies, which were unlikely to be based on representation by population principles. More generally, the national referendum on the Charlottetown Accord, held in October 1992, may have significantly influenced constitutional processes in the NWT. The demise of the accord, with its recognition of the inherent right to self government, raised questions about the overall climate for significant constitutional reform. Strategically, the outcome of the referendum highlighted the dangers in presenting to a cynical public, weary of deals struck by political elites, a complex interdependent set of constitutional proposals. Without genuine public consultation and involvement, people may – as they clearly did with the Charlottetown Accord – respond to a multi-faceted constitutional package on the basis of a negative reaction to individual provisions rather than on a balanced assessment of the overall set of proposals.

Such considerations led to delay on the Bourque recommendations and a rethinking of the process. The Committee of Political Leaders was broadened into a large Constitutional Development Steering Committee (CDSC), comprising the leaders or senior figures of the Dene Nation, the five regional Dene organizations, the Inuvialuit Regional Corporation, the Métis Nation of the NWT, the Native Women's Association of the NWT, as well as all 14 western MLAs, and three representatives of the Association of Western Tax-Based Municipalities (the mayors of Yellowknife, Hay River and Norman Wells, the three predominantly non-Aboriginal communities). It was understood that the CDSC would not formulate constitutional proposals on its own, but would direct and oversee extensive consultation processes, including two broadly-based constitutional conferences (the first to establish principles, the second to develop detailed provisions), a drafting process (possibly a constituent assembly or a committee of constitutional and legal experts) and a ratification procedure. After extensive discussion and delay, exacerbated by uncertainty about federal involvement and willingness to fund the process, the CDSC, in December 1993, approved a two-year workplan and set of substantive principles to guide the formulation of a new constitution.

With Ottawa's great potential to affect the direction of constitutional development in the west, it was thought essential that federal government representatives be closely involved with the CDSC process. No one wished to waste a substantial amount of the ever-dwindling time before division in thrashing out a constitution unacceptable to the federal government. Indian Affairs and Northern Development Minister Ron Irwin resisted an invitation to become a full member of the CDSC, since he did not wish the federal government to be perceived as leading this initiative, although federal officials were assigned to monitor the process closely. Early in 1994, Ottawa agreed to provide funding for the process, although not at the level sought by CDSC, and not without a commitment from the GNWT for a substantial financial contribution; thus, in addition to the $1 million from Ottawa, the CDSC received $500,000 from the GNWT.

Prior to this arrangement, the GNWT provided financial support to the CDSC so that its eight constituent organizations could research and develop their constitutional proposals; the position papers were published in August 1994. In the meantime, however, the Deh Cho and Treaty 8 leadership, and the Dene Nation, had pulled out of the CDSC process, citing it as "detrimental" to their interests, and had established a Treaty First Nation Committee to "promote and maintain the spirit and intent of Aboriginal and treaty sovereignty and facilitate the constitutional development of Denendeh."[41] This setback was not unexpected, although it did raise important questions about the effectiveness and the legitimacy of the process.

As a consequence of consistent federal and territorial support for the CDSC process as the only vehicle for constitutional discussion about the new western territory, the Deh Cho and Treaty 8 representatives agreed to return to the CDSC as observers. This afforded them access to funding for research and preparation of their constitutional position, as well as a broad forum to promote their positions advocating government based on Dene law and tradition.

Conflicting Constitutional Visions

What makes the task of forging agreement on constitutional principles for the Western Arctic such a daunting prospect is the nature of the disagreements. The expected conflicts over interests – boundaries, financial arrangements, composition of governing bodies and the like – are certainly present, but these could probably be resolved by compromise and mutual accommodation. More intractable are the often incompatible visions of the fundamental nature of governance, for example, Aboriginal self-government based on first nations' sovereignty *versus* public government on the southern provincial model, or strong, unified central government *versus* community-based government with little more than a hollow shell at the centre. This section highlights various groups' visions of how the Western NWT should be governed.

The Inuvialuit and the Gwich'in have put forward a joint proposal for constitutional reform in the West.[42] Their approach emphasizes a strong regional public government, although it notes that public and self-government arrangements can be compatible, and indeed anticipates self-government initiatives at the community level. The Western Arctic Regional Government that they envision would exercise "very wide ranging authority. It would hold many powers currently held by either the Government of the Northwest Territories or the Government of Canada."[43] Among its powers would be control over crown (public) lands and authority to tax these lands and their resources. Under this regime, the central territorial government would be left with little influence over what would amount to a virtually autonomous territory. An additional complication is the Inuvialuit and Gwich'in interest in acquiring constitutional protection for this scheme of governance under section 35 of the Constitution Act, 1982.

In terms of future directions for governance, the Sahtu Dene and Métis have made it clear that while they will participate actively in developing a western constitution, they accord higher priority to self-government negotiations with Ottawa. The Sahtu Tribal Council has declared that "a major aspiration which has not been *fully* addressed in the Land Claim is the capability of the Sahtu Dene and Métis to govern their own affairs as a distinct cultural identity within the framework of the federated state of Canada."[44] Sahtu negotiators unsuccessfully sought section 35 constitutional entrenchment for any self-government arrangements; their claim was settled before the Liberal government took office and proclaimed its acceptance of the inherent right, so that they now perceive greater latitude for pursuing self-government.[45] The Sahtu position paper in the Western constitutional process envisions considerable scope for public government, including education, taxation, economic development and social services, with Aboriginal government concentrating on wildlife harvesting and land management, although the division of powers it contemplates between public and Aboriginal governments clearly represents a preliminary view.[46] Moreover, many in the Sahtu apparently envision a substantial range of self-government responsibilities managed by and for Dene and Métis outside of territorial and community public governments. Reconciliation of such views with the commitment in the claim to "self-government within the framework of public government" will present negotiators with a significant challenge.

Similarly, the Sahtu position is marked by a particularly strong community focus: "[A]s far as the Sahtu is concerned, any practical expression of Aboriginal self-government, including a *Western Arctic Constitution, must recognize the community as the senior level of government.*"[47] The central territorial government, consisting of six MLAs and a small bureaucracy, would only hold the authority and jurisdiction granted it from the communities.

Claims negotiations currently underway between the Dogribs and the federal government differ in key respects from those which resulted in finalized claims in the northern regions of the Western Arctic. Given the Liberals' commitment to the inherent right, the Dogribs presume that the self-government agreements they may reach with Ottawa will have constitutional protection. Similarly, they believe their inherent right to self-government implies not co-management of lands and resources in their settlement area (as in the Inuvialuit, Gwich'in and Sahtu claims), but direct governing authority over it. While the Dogribs accept the need for public government and for a central territorial government, they place strong emphasis on extensive self-government and greatly enhanced community/regional government (at the expense of the central government). The Dogrib claim and the governance issues associated with it are complicated by uncertainties arising from territorial overlap between Dogrib and Treaty 8 lands. A formal reading of the treaties suggest that Dene living north of Great Slave Lake are covered by Treaty 11. Many Dene in the Yellowknife area, however, consider themselves part of the Treaty 8 groups south of the lake, and a solid historical-legal case can be made to support their view. In fact, the Yellowknives in Ndilo and Dettah, the communities near Yellowknife, are formally affiliated with the Treaty 8 Tribal Council and recognized as such by Ottawa.

Both in terms of claims and governance issues, the Treaty 8 Dene have adopted the most uncompromising position. They reject the federal government's comprehensive claims policy as a latter-day attempt to implement the infamous 1969 assimilationist white paper, and an abrogation of the spirit and intent of the treaty. Instead, they are pursuing treaty land entitlement negotiations with the federal government. This process would establish lands for the exclusive use of the Dene – in effect, reserves – in accordance with the treaty, without modifying its provisions or intent through the extinguishment of Aboriginal title, as required under the claims process.[48] While the federal government has accepted this approach and begun negotiations, a tremendous gap exists in the two sides' views as to the extent of land in question. Whereas the federal government's position is premised on the 160-acres-a-person formula of the treaty, the Treaty 8 Dene insist on substantial control, if not ownership of far greater amounts of land that encompass not only the Treaty 8 region in the NWT but also parts of the Treaty 8 region in Alberta and parts of the Dogrib, Sahtu and Inuit (Nunavut) areas.

Since they are not party to the treaty, the Métis in the Treaty 8 area are excluded from the treaty land entitlement process. However, in a major change in policy reflecting a desire to treat the Métis fairly, Ottawa has recently agreed to begin negotiations aimed at providing land and economic benefits for Métis in areas, such as the Treaty 8 lands, that would otherwise have been covered by comprehensive claims.

The Dene of Treaty 8 have not clearly specified how they want government to be structured, although the principles they have enunciated leave little doubt that it would be radically different from the current GNWT. In their view, "[T]he N.W.T. Treaty 8 First Nations were sovereign and have not relinquished their sovereignty...The Treaty has provided First Nations with recognition of their preexisting independence, laws, principles, and traditional forms of government."[49] They expect "a Tribal government exclusively based on Treaty 8 First Nations principles and values,"[50] exercising wide-ranging sovereignty. The clear, if not explicitly stated, implication is that Métis and non-Aboriginal people would have no role in such a government. As well, GNWT involvement in governing the Dene is rejected as undermining their sovereignty and independence; issues of governance are to be dealt with on a nation-to-nation basis with Canada.

Resolution of such fundamental questions – creating what would amount to a Dene territory in the southern NWT – remains highly uncertain, but on a more practical level, a process is emerging that would give Treaty 8 Dene greater control over day-to-day governmental concerns. Early in 1994, agreement was reached between the federal government, the GNWT and the Treaty 8 leadership to negotiate practical arrangements for Dene involvement in program administration and service delivery within their communities. Government functions currently provided by both Ottawa and the GNWT would be subject to transfer, along with existing levels of funding. The original idea, at least on the part of the federal and territorial governments, was the transfer of administrative responsibilities within a public government framework. As the process develops however, it is edging into the realm of self-government – contrary to what Ottawa and the GNWT initially contemplated. The Treaty 8 programs and services transfer process is unique, not only in the NWT but also in Canada. Although this exercise bears some resemblance to the Community Transfer Initiative, it does differ fundamentally in that CTI makes no distinction between services for Aboriginal and non-Aboriginal residents, whereas the Treaty 8 transfers would pertain only to Dene.

Dene leaders in the Deh Cho region concur in many of the positions adopted by the Treaty 8 First Nations: rejection of comprehensive claims, opposition to the CDSC process, denial of GNWT legitimacy and insistence on direct nation-to-nation dealings with Ottawa based on their inherent right of self-government. They envision realization of their inherent right through a constitutionally-entrenched Denendeh Act, which would create a new Denendeh Territory, in the southwest corner of the NWT.[51] Although they have stated that "we interpret our inherent right to government in terms of exclusive jurisdiction over our traditional lands of the Deh Cho,"[52] their views on governance differ in one fundamental respect from the Treaty 8 position. The Deh Cho Tribal Council has explicitly said that "the government of Denendeh will be a government for all residents in the Deh Cho."[53] Although some "special provisions" concerning matters that pertain to Aboriginal and treaty rights would protect Aboriginal interests, Dene and non-Aboriginal people would be full citizens of Denendeh with full political rights. The federal minister has indicated willingness to discuss the Deh Cho position, with a stipulation recognizing Ottawa's commitment to a single western territory.

The minister has also opened the door to a critical change in Ottawa's comprehensive claims policy, which could lead to fundamental adjustments in the stances of the Deh Cho and Treaty 8 Dene. In mid-November 1994, DIAND Minister Ron Irwin announced that he would be appointing a "fact finder" to review alternatives to extinguishment of Aboriginal land rights in the claims process. Since this requirement was pivotal in the rejection of the western NWT claim in 1990, a change in federal policy could result in a return to claims negotiations by groups unwilling to consider giving up their Aboriginal title to the land. That a workable alternative to extinguishment, satisfactory both to Ottawa and to Aboriginal people, can be developed is by no means certain; nor can its governance implications be easily divined. All the same, the potential this review holds for reshaping the political landscape of the western NWT is substantial.

Métis approaches to constitution building reflect the two principal features that distinguish the Métis from other Aboriginal peoples in the NWT. First, they are not covered by treaty, and thus lack the political protection and the land and resource entitlements treaties provide. Secondly, Métis live throughout the Western NWT, but constitute a majority in no region or community; thus, although the Métis are more numerous than several Aboriginal groups, their geographic dispersal leaves them politically vulnerable.

Among the principles informing the Métis constitutional position are insistence on the realization of Métis rights as Aboriginal people and on a Métis veto over constitutional changes that might affect them. In addition, although the Métis recognize that the Western Arctic comprises "districts and regions with diverse interests, concerns and ethnic populations" and that regional claims have created "*de facto* district governments in their respective areas," they argue for a strong central government.[54] This need is couched not in philosophical terms, but is put forward "in order to ensure representation of our [territorial] interests in southern Canada."[55]

No group or community in the NWT is unanimous in its political and constitutional views but the non-Aboriginal residents of the Western Arctic hold a particularly diverse range of opinions on their future political course. Moreover, whereas the leadership of the Aboriginal organizations routinely consults widely with its members and thus can for the most part fairly claim to speak on their behalf, it is difficult to identify authoritative spokespersons for non-Aboriginal people. Certainly, non-Aboriginal MLAs and municipal politicians consult their constituents extensively and the public statements of non-Aboriginal leaders reflect a substantial segment of public opinion. Yet it remains impossible to identify "the non-Aboriginal position" – if indeed a single, coherent position exists – in the way that the Gwich'in or Treaty 8 position can be identified.

In the CDSC process, the Association of Western Tax-Based Municipalities is seen as representing important elements of non-Aboriginal opinion, although, as noted, its views cannot be regarded as definitive. Moreover, the tax-based municipalities include both Aboriginal and non-Aboriginal residents, so that the Association's position must reflect this demographic reality. Not surprisingly, however, the AWTBM's constitutional stance differs fundamentally from the positions articulated by the Aboriginal groups in the CDSC process. For AWTBM, a strong central government is "both necessary and desirable." Consequently, "extreme care must be taken to avoid provisions in a new constitution which could result in fragmentation of the New Western Territory. It is not desirable to have a constitution which might, in effect, create several new "territories" within the Western Arctic."[56] The territorial model of governance favoured by AWTBM is very much one of public government. Thus, while accepting and affirming Aboriginal rights, whether existing or newly-recognized, AWTBM suggests that self-government should not be addressed in a new constitution, but rather "be left to the individual Aboriginal peoples to be decided in the forum they so choose."[57] Moreover, its proposals for the jurisdiction of the territorial government imply limited powers for district governments. Finally, AWTBM opposes the notion of guaranteed representation of groups or interests in the territorial legislature.

The wide gulfs separating the positions and approaches of the various groups involved in the CDSC process were front and centre when, after several postponements, the first Western Constitutional Conference took place in January 1995. Under the chairmanship of former Prime Minister Joe Clark, nearly 150 delegates convened in Yellowknife for four days of discussion on the principles to be incorporated into a new constitution. Half the delegates were elected officials (MLAs, mayors and councillors, band chiefs and councillors, Métis local presidents and the like); apart from the eight delegates nominated by interest groups (principally the CDSC organizations), the balance represented women's groups, youth and the public at large. Most delegates were long-time activists, with extensive experience in Aboriginal organizations or in territorial politics, but some were political neophytes or individuals without formal affiliation to any group, selected by their communities as public representatives. The GNWT was not formally represented *per se,* although all western MLAs and ministers took part as individual delegates on the same basis as other delegates. The federal government had observers present but was not an official participant. However, its presence was felt throughout the conference, not least because of a major policy statement delivered on the conference's first day by the Minister, Ron Irwin.

Many expected the conference to collapse under the weight of the seemingly intractable constitutional divisions facing the west. And indeed, the conference was barely under way when the NWT Treaty 8 Tribal Council withdrew from the proceedings, arguing "this process is a violation of our Treaty...[W]e do not give our consent to another government being formed which would try to control and to make laws, regulations and policies on our traditional lands."[58] In the end, however, the conference did not dissolve into competing political visions, but proved remarkably successful in fostering dialogue and understanding among all involved. The Deh Cho delegates who had come very close to walking out along with the Treaty 8 representatives were fulsome in their praise for the attitudes expressed during the conference, and even a Treaty 8 observer, at the end of the conference, spoke in cautiously optimistic terms about the progress registered.

While the importance of the spirit of accommodation and understanding generated at the conference should not be underestimated, the all-but-universal good feelings were largely achieved because no hard decisions had been taken and few clear principles agreed. The only substantive conclusion reached by the delegates was that Aboriginal self-government negotiations should be pursued, separately from the CDSC process, as a high priority matter with the federal government. Yet neither the nature of Aboriginal self-government nor its relation to a western constitutional order were specified. Similarly, the conference made no attempt to identify, let alone reconcile incompatible views on such issues as the interplay of Aboriginal and public government or the division of powers between the central and regional/community governments. Conference organizers and delegates, recognizing the complexity of these issues, realized that without detailed background information and clear, specific proposals, such discussions would be premature. CDSC was asked to see to this work, building on the foundation of the Bourque report, which emerged as a central reference point for conference delegates.

Thus, while important channels of communication were opened and understandings established as a basis for more focused deliberations, the challenge of transforming the very general agreements into workable structures of governance remains formidable. A second constitutional conference has been tentatively planned for early 1996, but is largely contingent on funding from Ottawa and from the GNWT, and on satisfactory progress on claims and self-government negotiations. Other stages in the process will be contingent on the progress achieved at this conference. However, the CDSC has pledged that the public will be afforded the opportunity to vote on whatever constitutional package emerges (though whether it is on a one-person, one-vote basis or adopts some weighting scheme to reduce Yellowknife's influence remains to be decided). Accordingly, in order to win the support of the non-Aboriginal population, some modification may be necessary so as to improve their representation in the process. Non-Aboriginal delegates were decidedly in the minority at the first CDSC conference. Moreover, as a group they lacked coherence and organization as well as institutional linkages to the population they were representing. By contrast, if the Aboriginal delegates were by no means monolithic in their views, they did caucus daily to develop strategy, and the Aboriginal organizations produced a joint statement at the end of the conference setting out what they saw as its central conclusions and the necessary next stages in the process. The point at issue is not whether the process treats the non-Aboriginal population fairly, but whether such a process can produce a set of constitutional proposals that the non-Aboriginal half of the western territory's population will support.

As illustrated by the withdrawals, at various times, of the Treaty 8 and Deh Cho groups, the CDSC process remains vulnerable and fragile. With groups coming to the table arguing constitutional positions from fundamentally different cultural and political starting points, the fact that it has endured and registered some considerable progress is a tribute to its members. Yet the prospect of the CDSC process successfully shaping a vision and a concrete set of proposals that can embrace these differing cultural values to the degree necessary to achieve popular ratification remains very much an open question.

Based on a review of the Charlottetown process, political scientist Michael Lusztig has recently argued that "the requirement of mass input into and legitimization of constitutional bargaining in deeply divided societies is incompatible with successful constitution making."[59] The public, he suggests, is typically unwilling to sanction the compromises that elites accept as necessary for reaching "mega constitutional" agreements. Moreover, the process of involving the public in constitutional development promotes "constitutional interest groups" that tend to seek special status and reject compromise. The western NWT is very much a divided society engaged in a process of mega constitutional change that not only seeks to include broad public involvement in the development of a comprehensive package of reforms, but also requires popular ratification of that package. CDSC strategists are fully aware of the problems Lusztig has identified, though their capacity to overcome them is highly uncertain.

Dilemmas Facing the Western Northwest Territories

The foregoing analysis of politics in the Western Arctic raises more questions than it answers. Not all issues of governance need to be resolved by the 1999 deadline for division, and doubtless government in the Western territory will evolve substantially following division. Nonetheless, very few residents of the West would accept continuation of the *status quo* that would result from constitutional stalemate. (Since the Nunavut Act makes provision for a western territorial government which is simply a scaled-down version of the existing structure, no legislative action would be required to perpetuate the current form of government in the western NWT.) The task of the political leaders of the Western Arctic is quite different from that facing the Nunavut leadership. In Nunavut, design of administrative institutions and processes, training and the construction of infrastructure are the key priorities; the basic form of government is not at issue in fundamental ways. By contrast, in the West, although transition to new forms of governing will certainly entail extensive planning, administrative arrangements are not the central concern; rather, the very nature of government has yet to be decided.

One measure of how fundamental are the issues to be resolved is the character of the constitutional discourse to date. By and large, the debate addresses the scope and nature of government, the definition of the political community and the basis of governmental legitimacy. Precious little attention has been devoted to questions that are typically paramount when constitutions are drawn up: questions relating to the form of government. Only occasional references may be found in the Bourque report and in the documents prepared by the participants in the CDSC process to design of legislative bodies (method of election, length of term and so on), their decision-making rules (simple majority, extraordinary majority, group veto), the locus of executive power (Westminster-style cabinet, directly-elected leader, collective consensual leadership, or other possibilities), and a host of other basic features of government. But, of course, when the very existence of a central government as anything more than a clearinghouse for federal cheques is open to debate, it is hardly surprising that consequential questions of this nature remain unanswered.

The most fundamental constitutional questions facing the Western NWT can be arrayed along two dimensions. The first set of issues concerns the balance between public government and Aboriginal self-government. In general terms, the more powers and responsibilities self-government regimes exercise, the less the scope for public government. The two are not inherently and entirely incompatible, and could certainly be integrated at the administrative and service delivery levels, if not necessarily at the level of political control and policy determination. Indeed, questions of the practical meshing of public and self-government will probably turn out to be more important than the "high politics" questions of formal division of power and jurisdiction. The other principal set of questions relates to the relative strength of the central and the district governments. If some degree of power-sharing (in terms not only of jurisdictions exclusive to one or other level but also in shared responsibilities) is inevitable, a fundamental conflict exists between two very different and clearly incompatible visions of government: strong, active central government *versus* powerful, autonomous regions with direct fiscal and legislative links to Ottawa. Further complications arise from the range of views on the primacy of community (as opposed to regional) government and indeed even the very desirability of regional government.

Since Aboriginal self-government is almost invariably rooted in a strong community focus, the two sets of issues – self-government *versus* public government, and the nature and degree of decentralization – are inextricably bound together, and thus must be resolved in tandem. And indeed, this is what is happening: for negotiations at the self-government tables are effectively reshaping public government, and doing so with a strong regional and community focus. At first blush, accommodating the sharply divergent principles and visions of government might appear an almost impossible challenge. Yet, while it will certainly be difficult, the prospects for a successful resolution are substantially enhanced by the all but universal expectation that the eventual constitutional regime will be highly asymmetrical, that is to say that political leaders throughout the western NWT presume that the balance between self-government and public government, the relationship between the central institutions and district or regional governments, and other key governance questions will not follow a single constitutional formula. Instead, they anticipate the emergence of quite different forms of government with quite different powers and responsibilities in different parts of the Western Arctic.

Resolution of the western imbroglio will not simply entail the various groups and interests negotiating in an attempt to modify their constitutional postures or to find common ground among them. The enumeration of the groups' positions in the previous section, which implicitly treated them as equals, offers a decidedly incomplete picture of the western constitutional landscape because it neglects the important roles of the GNWT and of Ottawa. Both are strong and influential, and neither is neutral.

The GNWT is a large, sophisticated organization, a pervasive force in the Western Arctic. Thus, the process of developing new political and governmental institutions for the West by no means begins with a clean slate, for the GNWT is already well entrenched and is generally unwilling to dismantle itself. Not only is the sheer weight of inertia a powerful ally of the GNWT, but the political and bureaucratic arms of the GNWT both call upon substantial resources and political influence. Though it accepts in principle both devolution of power to communities and the realization of self-government arrangements, as the limited success of the CTI has shown, in practical terms, the GNWT has not realized great progress toward these goals. All told, the GNWT is a powerful force for the retention of extensive public government, one with strong central institutions.

An even more significant force is the federal government, which retains an absolutely critical role in the political development of the Western territory. Ottawa's consent will be required to implement any constitutional agreements that go beyond mere delegation or sharing of existing territorial powers – as they almost certainly will. As well, the capacity and willingness of the federal government to finance the additional costs that will inevitably arise from new levels and structures of government will also be an issue.

Ottawa has the capacity to assume a very active role in shaping government in the western NWT. If it chose to sanction far-reaching self-government agreements with stand-alone Aboriginal institutions for the delivery of programs and services exclusively to Aboriginal people, for example, the federal government could effectively render the CDSC process meaningless and severely undercut the authority of the GNWT. Conversely, Ottawa can serve as a powerful supporter of the GNWT (or its western successor). And indeed, Ottawa's preference has been clear for some time, as its submission to the Royal Commission on Aboriginal Peoples noted: "Strengthening of public government in the North through territorial governments is a high priority of the federal government, which sees it as an appropriate democratic institutional framework for the social and economic development of Aboriginal and Non-Aboriginal peoples residing in Canada's northern regions."[60]

Northerners, for many of whom the federal government is necessarily a remote, abstract construct, tend to view it as a monolith with uniform views and policies. Effectively, however, several "Ottawas" exist: the priorities and views of the Department of Indian Affairs and Northern Development may differ significantly from those of the Department of Finance, which in turn may not be those of the Department of Justice or the Treasury Board. Interdepartmental politics in Ottawa has historically had, and will doubtless continue to have, far-reaching effects on northern political development.

Like other Canadians, northerners tend to be preoccupied with their own problems, and can thus lose sight of the fact that the federal government – and its component departments, such as DIAND – has a great many issues and problems competing for priority attention. With Aboriginal groups across Canada pressing for resolution of their land claims, self-government demands and other grievances, only a fraction of the minister's time (and a much smaller fraction of Cabinet's time) can be devoted to northern concerns. Nor does Ottawa formulate policy toward the North without regard for consequences elsewhere in Canada; in other words, the federal government may hesitate to agree to policies it believes appropriate for the North for fear of setting precedents that it would have to match in other parts of Canada. By way of illustration, federal policy on the form that an Inuit homeland in Nunavut would take was for years clearly shaped by concerns as to the consequences that establishing an "ethnic" territory might have for Quebec's constitutional demands. Similarly, agreements that Ottawa might reach on melding public and Aboriginal self-government in the Western NWT would doubtless influence self-government negotiations in southern Canada. In short, Ottawa's stance on the appropriate course of political development in the western NWT necessarily reflects a complex, sometimes contradictory set of policy imperatives and competing political priorities.

Recent federal policy on the constitutional future of the western NWT has not been to impose specific solutions, but to let northerners work out their own solutions to their problems. At the same time, Ottawa has clearly specified some basic limits on the nature and form of government it is prepared to countenance. In his address to the January 1995 CDSC Conference, Ron Irwin explicitly ruled out the idea, promoted by various Aboriginal organizations, of dividing the western NWT into two or more territories, as well as the related possibility of an extreme decentralization of power to regional or district governments:

Here in the Western Territory, the Government of Canada supports, as does the Government of the Northwest Territories, the concept of one Territorial government...[A] single territorial government in the west is the way to ensure effective government...[A] single territorial government does not mean that people cannot have control over regional or local interests. I support decentralization when it is consistent with good government and fiscal responsibility...[A]t the same time, given fiscal realities, we simply cannot create a proliferation of independent government structures.[61]

While the minister reaffirmed the Liberal government's commitment to recognizing the inherent right of self-government, he firmly enunciated its position that "the inherent right of self-government should find expression primarily through the public government and be implemented in partnership with the federal and territorial governments." He also spelled out conditions relating to process: on the one hand, "participation of Aboriginal people in building government structures for the Western Territory is essential...if they are not participating, there will be no process"; on the other hand, "working out self-government arrangements...[requires] full and direct involvement of the Territorial government at the negotiating table."[62]

Since the need for a western constitutional settlement has again come to the political fore in the 1990s, Ottawa has generally avoided actions that might foreclose any realistic constitutional options. The federal government's desire for strong and effective public government is nonetheless evident in its continued willingness to negotiate a "northern accord" to transfer jurisdiction for non-renewable resources to the GNWT, despite significant opposition from Aboriginal groups. Moreover, Ottawa's interest in bringing forward a Mackenzie Valley Resource Management Act is a further indication of its support for public government institutions with territorial scope. The agencies proposed under the bill would promote coordination of effort and coherence of policy among the various wildlife management, environmental oversight and resource development boards established by claims or through other means in the Western Arctic. Aboriginal organizations have criticized the proposed bill as pre-empting important self-government initiatives; the GNWT has taken an active interest in the consultations on the draft bill.

Conclusion

The previous chapter, on the Yukon, concluded by noting manifold uncertainties about the practical working relations between the Yukon government and the governments of the various Yukon First Nations. Similar uncertainties only mark the starting point for considering the future political shape of the western NWT. A principal theme of this chapter has been the enormous difficulty of reconciling public and Aboriginal self-government in the NWT. What makes the prospect of bridging this gulf so daunting is the recognition that not simply practical questions of distribution of powers are at issue, but that quite fundamental conceptions of governance underpin the different governmental forms and processes preferred by various groups. If it is true that individual First Nations in the Yukon are establishing different governmental systems, with differing relations to the territorial government, it is also true that a far wider range of variation on key governance issues are likely to emerge among the regions and groups in the western NWT.

The federal government will exert strong influence on how government in the western NWT unfolds, in particular through its preference for a single, effective public territorial government. At the very least, however, a high degree of asymmetry will mark the linkages between the central territorial government and the regions and Aboriginal governments. Significant variations can be expected across governments with respect to relations with Ottawa, the political status of the Métis, the absence or presence of settled land claims (and the status of the public government bodies established by the claims for co-management of land and resources), the political role of non-Aboriginal people, the extent of the jurisdictional transfer of self-government authority to Aboriginal groups, the compatibility of public and self-government institutions, the relative authority of regional and community governments. As in the Yukon, the federal government's willingness to fund northern government, along with territorial residents' acceptance of the need to raise additional revenue from local sources, will be critical factors in shaping the various orders and forms of government.

Much of the political development in the NWT over the past three decades has occurred in an *ad hoc,* unplanned manner or, in the case of the changes wrought by the Carrothers and Drury reports, through plans which took insufficient account of Aboriginal values and approaches to governance. The structures of government that emerge from the current constitutional process will, by contrast, be carefully designed, with Aboriginal interests and modes of governance very much at the forefront. On a different plane, even the structures of public government – both at the territorial and local/regional levels – will be specifically developed with northern needs and outlooks in mind. Thus, the Westminster cabinet-parliamentary system, which was imposed on the NWT without consultation or acceptance by northerners, may well be rejected altogether (rather than simply modified in important ways, as at present) in favour of radically different forms of government. By way of illustration, the government of the new western territory might include guaranteed representation and veto powers for various Aboriginal groups; it might be based on direct election of the government leader or a series of committees responsible for policy development and administration (both of which are incompatible with British-style responsible government); it might consist of little more than a loose confederal structure, with effective power lodged at the regional or community level; and it could incorporate a range of mechanisms for melding public and Aboriginal self-government.

In working toward a new political order, the desire to lash out at the current institutional forms will doubtless tempt the people of the western territory to do away with existing structures and processes. Given the often high levels of frustration and distaste for how the GNWT is structured and operates, this is understandable. Yet institutions should be jettisoned only when better alternatives are available, not because they fail to live up fully to expectations. Proposed changes should be thought through carefully to ensure not only that they will indeed rectify the weaknesses in the existing regime but also that they do not generate more problems than they solve. Widespread disaffection with the behaviour of public government politicians, for example, carries over into a largely-unexamined presumption that the essential flaw lies in the "consensus government" system. Comparisons of "consensus government" tend to measure it against an ideal of how government should work rather than against real-life alternatives. Similarly, the perceived lack of coherent policy direction and accountability in the GNWT cabinet and the legislature has given rise to calls for direct, universal election of the premier. Such a change would impose greater coherence and discipline on the government by dramatically enhancing the premier's power, but it would also bring other, perhaps less palatable consequences, including far-reaching centralization of power and a much increased likelihood of party politics.[63] Finally, the undoubted benefits of decentralizing power from the Yellowknife apparatus and moving it closer to the people in the form of community and regional governments must be balanced with a recognition of the essential roles that an effective central government alone can play. Only through a central government can economies of scale be realized, policy on territory-wide concerns coordinated, revenue sharing regimes developed and a strong, unified voice heard in dealings with Ottawa and with the provinces.

Division will change forever the northern political landscape. In one sense, the departure of the Inuit with the creation of Nunavut will remove an important set of complexities from the politics of the western NWT. No longer will the need to balance eastern and western interests or the need to accommodate Inuit aspirations and cultural imperatives loom as central political considerations. However, by eliminating these complexities, division may emphasize the fundamental contrasts between and among Aboriginal and non-Aboriginal people in the western territory and heighten the potential for political conflict (particularly in light of the limited financial resources available). A more positive interpretation would see division as forcing all residents of the western NWT to come to terms with the political and financial constraints they all face in ways that take into account all cultures, perspectives and interests.

Notes

1. Unless otherwise indicated, all population and demographic figures are taken or calculated from Statistics Canada, *Canada's Aboriginal Population by Census Subdivisions and Census Metropolitan Areas*, Catalogue 94-326, March 1994, table 1.

2. John Pollard, *Northwest Territories 1994-95 Budget Address*, p. 35.

3. See Robert M. Bone, *The Geography of the Canadian North* (Toronto: Oxford University Press, 1992), p. 214.

4. Peter Gardner, "Aboriginal Community Incomes and Migration in the NWT: Policy Issues and Alternatives," *Canadian Public Policy*, Vol. 20, no. 3 (September 1994), p. 301.

5. Ethnographically and linguistically, the small number of Cree, who are concentrated in the Fort Smith area, are not Dene, although they do belong to the Dene Nation. Politically, this is not a meaningful distinction.

6. Although all Métis are of mixed blood, not all mixed blood are Métis; the distinction between Dene and Métis tends to reflect legal categories based on historical idiosyncracies rather than ancestry.

7. Gordon Robertson, *Northern Provinces: A Mistaken Goal* (Montreal: Institute for Research on Public Policy, 1985), p. viii.

8. Advisory Commission on the Development in the Northwest Territories, *Report* (Ottawa, 1966).

9. Kerry Abel, *Drum Songs: Glimpses of Dene History* (Montreal: McGill-Queen's University Press, 1993), p. 244.

10. "The Dene Declaration," reprinted in Mel Watkins (ed.), *Dene Nation: The Colony Within* (Toronto: University of Toronto Press, 1977), p. 4.

11. Special Representative for Constitutional Development in the Northwest Territories, *Constitutional Development in the Northwest Territories* (Ottawa: Supply and Services Canada, 1979).

12. "Aboriginal Organizations Unite to Oppose Northern Accord," press release, undated (July 28, 1994?). Representatives of the Treaty 8 First Nations, the Deh Cho Council, the Dogrib Treaty 11 Council and the Gwich'in Tribal Council agreed to the statement in the press release. These sentiments were repeatedly emphasized by Aboriginal representatives at the January 1995 Constitutional Conference in Yellowknife.

13. "Minister Irwin Announces Results of DIAND Program Review," News Release, February 27, 1995, p. 2.

14. Projections for 1995-96 indicated that $1005 million of the GNWT's $1213 million in revenue were to come from the federal government (though not all by way of formula funding); John Pollard, *Northwest Territories 1995-96 Budget Address*, February 20, 1995, p. 22.

15. Statement by John Pollard, Minister of Finance, Legislative Assembly of the Northwest Territories, *Hansard Offical Report*, March 23, 1993, p. 1092.

16. At the time of writing, negotiations on a new formula agreement were still under way. Although the previous agreement expired March 31, 1995, it was, in accordance with provisions in the agreement, automatically extended on an interim basis.

17. Pollard, *Budget Address*, p. 1.

18. Paul Martin, Minister of Finance, *Budget Speech*, February 27, 1995, p. 19.

19. Marina Devine, "Budget bad news for GNWT: Pollard," *Nunatsiaq News*, March 3, 1995, p. 2. This would not be an actual cut of $50 million, but a reduction in the amount by which the transfer to the GNWT would be expected to grow.

20. Although backroom politicking remains critical, important elements of the process now take place in public in a "Territorial Leadership Committee," which is in effect an unofficial session of the House.

21. In formal terms, MLAs have only removed one minister from Cabinet, in 1987; in addition, however, two ministers who resigned late in 1992 would almost certainly have been removed by the MLAs had they not resigned.

22. Until recently, the first minister in the NWT was generally known as the "government leader"; in 1994, the territorial Assembly formally authorized the term "premier," which was already coming into common use.

23. That this is a pragmatic rather than an ideological response is suggested by the acceptance and the primacy of political parties in national politics among Aboriginal people, including Aboriginal MLAs who run as independents in territorial elections.

24. Government of the Northwest Territories, *1992 and 1993 Public Service Annual Report*, p. 16. This figure includes teachers, nursing staff, social workers and others who, in the south, would not be directly employed by provincial governments.

25. Legislative Assembly of the Northwest Territories, *Hansard Offical Report*, March 24, 1992, p. 419.

26. Regional and Tribal Councils Review Coordinating Committee, *Report on Regional and Tribal Councils in the Northwest Territories* (Yellowknife, 1987).

27. The Inuit claim and the Nunavut government are discussed in chapter 4.

28. Indian and Northern Affairs Canada, *Comprehensive Land Claims Policy* (Ottawa, 1987), p. 18.

29. The Liberal Party's "Red Book" of campaign promises in the 1993 election included the following commitment: "A Liberal government will act on the premise that the inherent right of self-government is an existing Aboriginal and treaty right." Liberal Party of Canada, *Creating Opportunity: The Liberal Plan for Canada*, 1993, p. 98.

30. *Inuvialuit Final Agreement*, 1984, s. 4 (3).

31. "Western Arctic Regional Government: Inuvialuit and Gwich'in Proposal for Reshaping Government in the Western Arctic, November, 1993," in Western Northwest Territories Constitutional Development Steering Committee, *Member Group Research Reports* (August 1994), pp. 4-5.

32. Indian and Northern Affairs Canada, *The Evolution of Public Governments in the North and the Implications for Aboriginal Peoples* (February 1993), p. 27.

33. Quoted in Indian and Northern Affairs Canada, *The Evolution of Public Governments in the North*, p. 27.

34. Quoted in James Hrynyshn, "Yukon Vows to Fight Gwich'in Claim," *News/North*, July 22, 1991, p. 3.

35. Inuvialuit Final Agreement, s. 2.

36. *Gwich'in Comprehensive Land Claim Agreement*, 1992, s. 2.1.1; *Sahtu Dene and Métis Comprehensive Land Claim Agreement*, 1993, s. 2.1.1.

37. Gwich'in Final Agreement, ss. 5.1.1 and 5.1.10; the Sahtu Dene and Métis Final Agreement contains virtually identical language.

38. Gwich'in Final Agreement, Appendix B, ss. 1.1, 1.3. The Sahtu claim contains identical language.

39. Commission for Constitutional Development, *Working Toward A Common Future* (Yellowknife, April 1992), p. 21.

40. Commission for Constitutional Development, *Working Toward A Common Future*, p. 25.

41. "Statement of Dene Nation," January 26, 1994.

42. "Western Arctic Regional Government: Inuvialuit and Gwich'in Proposal for Reshaping Government in the Western Arctic," in Western Northwest Territories Constitutional Development Steering Committee, *Member Group Research Reports*.

43. "Western Arctic Regional Government," p. 9.

44. Sahtu Tribal Council, "Work Project for the Constitutional Development Steering Committee Working Group," in Western Northwest Territories Constitutional Development Steering Committee, *Member Group Research Reports*, p. 2.

45. The legislation finalizing the Sahtu claim was passed after the Liberals came to power, but its provisions had been determined by the previous Conservative government.

46. Sahtu Tribal Council, "Work Project," pp. 11-12.

47. Sahtu Tribal Council, "Work Project," p. 5. Emphasis in original.

48. Because the pressure for development of the land was far less severe than on the Prairies, where the reserve system became dominant, few reserves (and only one of significance, at Hay River) have been established in the NWT.

49. François Paulette and Wendy Aasen, "Synopsis of Protocol: Nationhood (Treaty 8 First Nations) within a New Western Territory (N.W.T. Act)," interim report on constitutional development (September 1993), p. 13.

50. Paulette and Aasen, "Synopsis of Protocol," p. 11.

51. "Summary of the Principles of the Constitution of Denendeh," appended to Deh Cho Tribal Council, "Requirements for the Settlement of Dene Government in the Northwest Territories," in WNT Constitutional Development Steering Committee, *Member Group Research Reports*, section I.

52. Deh Cho Tribal Council, "Requirements," p. 3.

53. "Principles," section II.

54. Métis Nation – Northwest Territories, "A Discussion Paper on Constitutional Development in a New Western Territory," in WNT Constitutional Development Steering Committee, *Member Group Research Reports*, p. 4.

55. Métis Nation – Northwest Territories, "Discussion Paper," p. 4.

56. Association of Western Tax-Based Municipalities, "Discussion Paper on a Constitution for the New Western Territory," WNT Constitutional Development Steering Committee, *Member Group Research Reports*, pp. 2-3.

57. Association of Western Tax-Based Municipalities, "Discussion Paper," p. 38.

58. Treaty 8 Tribal Council "Statement to Constitutional Development Steering Committee," January 18, 1995.

59. Michael Lusztig, "Constitutional Paralysis: Why Canadian Constitutional Initiatives Are Doomed to Fail," *Canadian Journal of Political Science*, Vol. 27, no. 4 (December 1994), p. 748.

60. Indian Affairs and Northern Development Canada, *The Evolution of Public Governments in the North*, p. ii.

61. Ron Irwin, "Speech to Conference," in Constitutional Development Steering Committee, *Conference Report: First Constitutional Conference*, Western NWT (Yellowknife, 1995), pp. 8-9.

62. Irwin, "Speech to Conference," p. 11.

63. Direct election of the premier is discussed in Brian Lewis, "Choosing a Premier –Responsible to the Northwest Territories House or Its People?" *The Parliamentarian*, Vol. 75, no. 3 (July 1994), pp. C-16, C-18; and Graham White, "Consequences of Electing the Government Leader of the Northwest Territories," paper prepared for the Strategic Planning Session of the Northwest Territories Legislative Assembly, Cambridge Bay, NWT, October 1993.

Four

Getting to Nunavut

Introduction

> Creation of a Nunavut Territory and Government has been an Inuit goal
> for almost 20 years...We are pleased to be turning dreams into reality.[1]

These were the words of James Eetoolook, acting President of the
Tungavik Federation of Nunavut, on October 30, 1992, at the historic
signing of the Nunavut Political Accord in Iqaluit. The Accord represented, on the one hand, the conclusion of a long process of negotiation
between Canada and the Inuit people of the central and Eastern Arctic,
and, on the other, the start of an extensive process of change that will
culminate in 1999 with the division of the NWT into a new, as yet
unnamed western territory and the new eastern territory of Nunavut.

Nunavut's society and economy are outlined in chapter 3, as are current political issues and governmental structures in the NWT. However,
the debate and the process leading to the creation of Canada's newest
"proto-province," and the principal features of the Nunavut government
deserve special treatment.

Accordingly, this chapter describes the political debate surrounding
the creation of the new territory of Nunavut which, under the Nunavut
Act, must be established by April 1, 1999. The instruments to create the
new territory – the Nunavut land claim settlement, the Nunavut Political

Accord (the political agreement between the Inuit, the Government of Canada and the Government of the Northwest Territories) and the Nunavut Act – are discussed. Another principal focus is the planning and implementation framework through which the new territory and its government will come into being. The chapter concludes with a discussion of Nunavut within the larger Canadian context.

Overview

The creation of Nunavut is inextricably bound up with, and indeed is a direct consequence of, the resolution of the Inuit land claim. In all comprehensive land claims in northern Canada, claimant groups have attempted to link settlement of land ownership and control issues to self-government. The Inuit, however, have managed to achieve far more of their governmental aspirations through the claims process than any other Aboriginal group.

Several factors underlie this unique Inuit success. Unlike the situation in the Western NWT, the land occupied by the Inuit in the central and Eastern Arctic was never subject to treaties with either the British or Canadian government. In addition, two oft-noted aspects of the Inuit character, patient determination and pragmatism, contributed to the eventual outcome. Throughout an exceedingly protracted negotiation process, in which they often seemed to have met impenetrable barriers, the Inuit never lost sight of their fundamental goal: an Inuit homeland to protect and nurture Inuit culture. Their pragmatism was evident in their willingness to look beyond symbolic issues (such as the colonial origin of existing government structures) and to accept a governmental formula – public government, very much on the current GNWT model – that would be effective in meeting their political objectives. Of course, this approach was possible because of the unique demographics of Nunavut, with its large Aboriginal majority (more than 80 percent of Nunavut residents are Inuit, and this numerical dominance seems unlikely to change in the foreseeable future). Moreover, although regional antagonisms certainly exist in Nunavut, as signified in the various region dialects of Inuktitut, the Inuit are far less beset by divisions than are the Dene-Métis of the Western NWT. This relative social homogeneity in turn makes for a political situation far less complex than that in the Western Arctic.

The land and financial components of the claim are broadly similar to other settled claims in the North. They provide the Inuit with a substantial land base, monetary payments and a significant role in resource management.

Map 3: Nunavut

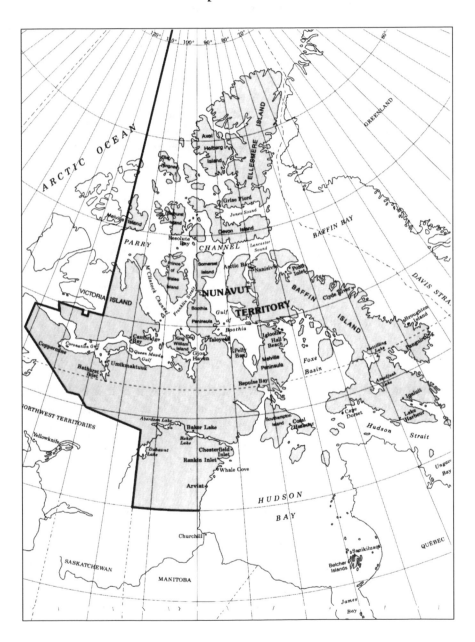

Source: JLC Repro Graphic Inc., Ottawa

The claim establishes an Inuit settlement region of two million square kilometres, with direct Inuit ownership of 350,000 square kilometres (with subsurface rights to 36,000 square kilometres) in the central and Eastern Arctic. The cash settlement for the 17,500 beneficiaries is $1.14 billion over 14 years, with an additional $13 million in the form of a training trust fund. The claim also guarantees Inuit involvement on a range of resource management boards (land, water, wildlife and environment) that will render decisions throughout the settlement region and Nunavut.[2]

Finally, the claim included a commitment from Canada to establish a separate Nunavut territory, with effective Inuit control over a full range of provincial-type responsibilities. Other northern claims have included general commitments to negotiate self-government arrangements within very broad frameworks, but none incorporates anything like the clear, firm commitment to create Nunavut. To an important extent, the federal government's acceptance, through the claim, of the principle of a Nunavut government reflected the Inuit decision to follow a public, rather than Aboriginal self-government model. Some Dene leaders in the Western NWT believe that the Inuit gave away far too much in accepting a public government rather than an Aboriginal self-government regime, but this does not appear to be a concern for Inuit leaders.

Background to the Claim and Division

The possibility of dividing the NWT along east-west lines was first discussed in the period 1959 to 1963, with debate in the Territorial Council on establishing a separate Mackenzie Territory for the western NWT. Inuit aspirations were not of concern in this debate. Indeed, quite the opposite was true, since the principal argument favouring division was that freeing the Western NWT from the constraining influence of the more "backward" Eastern Arctic would allow a smaller western territory to progress more rapidly in its political development. A sympathetic federal government introduced legislation in the House of Commons that would have created the new territories of Mackenzie in the west and Nunassiaq in the east. At the committee stage in the Commons, however, it became apparent that the prime impetus for division came from the federally appointed members of a Territorial Council that had no representatives – elected or appointed – from the Eastern Arctic, nor support from the people of either the western or eastern regions of the NWT. With the dissolution of Parliament in 1963 the bills died on the *Order Paper.*

Subsequently, the 1966 report of the Advisory Commission on the Development of Government in the NWT acknowledged that division of the NWT was probably inevitable but did not recommend its immediate implementation.[3] Commissioner A.W.R. Carrothers argued that division would effectively isolate the Inuit, leaving them vulnerable to unilateral action by Ottawa on political and economic development. His preference was to extend the franchise to include the eastern NWT so that "residents of the east would have the same opportunities as those in the west of participating in their government...In short, representation now, possible division later."[4]

Despite initiatives to encourage the political empowerment of Inuit in the process of government, the reality of having the institutions of government in the east directed from Yellowknife did not ensure sufficient sensitivity to eastern concerns. In the late 1960s and early 1970s, the physical, psychological and cultural remoteness of the GNWT figured prominently in Inuit proposals for land claims and political self-determination.

In common with Aboriginal people throughout Canada, the Inuit developed detailed and far-reaching land claims in the 1970s which, following the landmark 1973 Calder case, the federal government agreed to accept as a basis for negotiation. In 1976 the Inuit Tapirisat of Canada (ITC), representing Inuit throughout Canada, submitted a formal proposal to Prime Minister Trudeau for the settlement of the Inuit land claim. The Inuit position paper argued for the creation of Nunavut. This would remain a foundation principle of the Inuit throughout the entire claims process. For the ITC, a basic goal was to "preserve Inuit identity and the traditional way-of-life so far as possible; "this could be achieved by "the creation of Nunavut Territory, in respect to which through numbers and voting power, the Inuit will have control for the foreseeable future."[5] The ITC paper argued that "the basic idea is to create a Territory, the vast majority of the people within which, will be Inuit. As such, this Territory and its institutions will better reflect Inuit values and perspectives than with the present Northwest Territories."[6]

Although this initial proposal was formally withdrawn by the ITC, its call for division remained a fundamental component of the Inuit position. Subsequent Inuit declarations and position papers, such as the 1979 *Political Development in Nunavut,* refined and elaborated various aspects of the claim and the Nunavut proposal, but never wavered from the fundamental premise that settlement of the claim would require the establishment of Nunavut.

The late 1970s and early 1980s witnessed both setbacks and progress for the Inuit. Reflecting the Aboriginal majority on the Territorial Council, the GNWT became notably more sympathetic to Inuit aspirations and to the notion of dividing the NWT. The non-Inuit in the western and central NWT became increasingly aware and interested in the idea of Nunavut. National constitutional processes, which led to fundamental revision of Canada's constitution in 1982 (including constitutional entrenchment of Aboriginal rights, although in undefined form), also contributed to a climate favourable to adventurous constitutional departures.

The Inuit had created new organizations to pursue their claims, and while some advances were registered, progress in formal negotiations with Ottawa was discouragingly slow. In addition, the Inuvialuit of the northwest NWT, who had originally been party to the ITC Nunavut proposal, chose to pursue separate land claims negotiations with the federal government. The Inuvialuit, facing intense pressure from oil and gas development in the Beaufort Sea, believed they could not afford to wait until the entire Inuit claim was resolved to protect their interests. Moreover, the Inuvialuit's economic and communications ties to the Mackenzie Valley were stronger than those with the Inuit communities to the east. The departure of the Inuvialuit from the Inuit claimant groups, and the settlement of their claim in 1984, also meant that the resource-rich Beaufort region would eventually become part of a western territory rather than of Nunavut.

A number of key developments occurred in 1982, most notably a plebiscite on division of the NWT. Given the critical link between the Inuit land claim proposal and the creation of a new territory, this was an essential step. In the plebiscite, people were asked if they favoured the idea of division, but specific proposals or boundaries were not offered. The concept received hesitant support from the NWT population: of the 53 percent of the population who turned out to the polls, 56 percent voted in favour of division. Not surprisingly, support was strong in the eastern and central Artic Inuit communities. The western mixed Dene/non-Aboriginal communities were reluctant to support a concept whose implications and benefits for them were far from clear. At the same time, Aboriginal voters of the western NWT did not wish to block Inuit efforts toward self-determination; accordingly, they gave stronger support to division than did non-Aboriginal residents of the NWT.

During 1982, a new Inuit organization, the Tungavik Federation of Nunavut (TFN), was established to focus exclusively on the Nunavut claim and associated matters. It was "an independent and [compared to previous, ITC-linked bodies] more broadly based coalition of Inuit organizations having separate corporate status."[7]

In February of the same year, the Constitutional Alliance of the NWT was formed by a number of Territorial Council members and Aboriginal leaders who believed a detailed debate and planning process was essential if division were to occur. In July the Alliance established two subgroups, the Nunavut Constitutional Forum (NCF) and the Western Constitutional Forum (WCF), to represent the respective interests of east and west. In November, the Minister of Indian Affairs and Northern Development, John Munro, announced that federal support for division was conditional upon continued popular support across the NWT, settlement of land claims, agreement on a boundary and achievement of a consensus on the division of powers for the territorial, regional and community levels of government.

During the remaining years of the decade, there were periods of substantial achievement and of stalemate. A key indicator of the prospects for Nunavut was the boundary question, which proved a particularly difficult hurdle. It was generally accepted that the Nunavut boundary would roughly follow the tree-line, but both Inuit and Dene claimed extensive tracts of land in the central Arctic as traditional hunting areas.[8] Despite attempts to work out compromises through overlapping usage zones and other means, voluntary settlement of the boundary proved impossible. A tentative boundary agreement reached in 1985 fell apart, as did the 1987 Iqaluit Agreement between the NCF and WCF, which for a time appeared to have settled the key issues standing in the way of division. The Iqaluit Agreement was abandoned owing to the dissatisfaction of the Dene-Métis in the Western NWT and of some people in the Kitikmeot (central Arctic) and Inuvialuit regions with the proposed boundary.

Without a settled boundary, Nunavut could not proceed, since it was necessary to delineate both the Inuit settlement area and the border of Nunavut. In 1991, the federal government appointed a former Commissioner of the NWT, John Parker, to consult those affected and recommend a boundary. The Inuit generally accepted the boundary he proposed, but the Dene and Métis thought that it ran too far to the west (that is, into what they believed to be their lands). The federal minister, however, made it clear that the "Parker line" might be entirely accepted or rejected, but that if there were to be an east-west boundary, this was it. A May 1992 plebiscite put the issue before the territorial electorate. Technically, this was a vote strictly on the boundary proposed by Parker, but it was widely felt that the vote would also signal reaffirmation or rejection of the concept of division. The outcome was reminiscent of 1982, with a relatively low turnout and a narrow majority – 54 percent – voting to accept the line. Whereas the Nunavut region was overwhelmingly in support (nine to one in favour), the people of the west voted three to one against the boundary line (but failed to turn out in sufficient numbers to defeat the proposal). Following this narrow victory, Ottawa, the GNWT and the Inuit announced their continued commitment to moving forward with division.

Nunavut Becomes a Reality

While the Parker review was under way and the boundary vote being organized, negotiators reached first an agreement-in-principle on the Inuit land claim and, subsequently, in December 1991, a draft final agreement. The boundary question remained a critical outstanding issue, but it was by no means the only problem to be addressed. With the narrow public acceptance in the 1992 plebiscite, the boundary hurdle was removed and attention became focused on the difficult task of securing an acceptable process for division. This was not simply a question of boundaries, for it raised broad constitutional issues.

The Inuit framed their case for Nunavut as an expression of their claims and, by extension, of their self-government interests. They wished to see the concept of Nunavut as a separate territory incorporated into the land claim itself. By so doing, the Inuit and the federal government would be agreeing to the recognition of the new territory as an embodiment of the Inuit's Aboriginal rights, protected by section 35 of the Constitution Act, 1982.

This, the federal government's negotiators argued, would give the territory an unacceptable constitutional status, considering that Nunavut was to be a public government representing, serving and including all Canadians living in that area, not just the Inuit. From Ottawa's perspective it would be inappropriate to use a land claim with an Aboriginal group as the instrument to establish a public government.

Ottawa maintained that a new territory and its public government would have to be created through a separate act of Parliament, not through an ethnically-based land claim agreement recognized and protected by the Constitution. Nunavut's existence would have to stand apart from the claim because of its relationship to the general interests of all Canadians and the democratic principles of the federation.

A compromise acceptable to all parties was struck through a provision in the claim committing Canada to negotiate a "Nunavut Political Accord" that would not stand as a formal part of the claim but would effectively provide for the creation of Nunavut. Thus article 4 of the TFN Land Claims Agreement stipulates:

> The Government of Canada will recommend to Parliament, as a government measure, legislation to establish, within a defined time period, a new Nunavut Territory, with its own Legislative Assembly and public government, separate from the government of the remainder of the Northwest Territories.
>
> Therefore, Canada and the Territorial Government and Tungavik Federation of Nunavut shall negotiate a political Accord to deal with the establishment of Nunavut...
>
> Neither the said political accord nor any legislation enacted pursuant to the political accord shall accompany or form part of this Agreement or any legislation ratifying this Agreement. Neither the said political accord nor anything in the legislation enacted pursuant to the political accord is intended to be a land claims agreement or treaty right within the meaning of Section 35 of the *Constitution Act, 1982.*[9]

Negotiation of the Nunavut Political Accord took only six months. This remarkable speed was due to Ottawa's assessment that the Inuit demands were essentially reasonable and the relative lack of major points of contention. The elements of the Accord reflect the practical and reasonable approach taken by the Inuit. The Accord speaks to an interest in federal legislation for Nunavut "similar to the present Northwest Territories Act with such modernization and clarification as may be appropriate" (section 2.1). It specifies that the "types of powers of the Nunavut Legislative Assembly and Nunavut Government shall be generally consistent with those in the present Northwest Territories Act" (section 4.1). Essentially, the Inuit were prepared to accept a modified *status quo,* with the critical difference that they, not a distant government in Yellowknife, would be in control.[10]

A small but telling point about the Inuit approach to Nunavut is that neither the Nunavut Political Accord nor the Nunavut Act makes any reference to "citizens" of Nunavut. This contrasts with the self-government agreements finalized under the Council of Yukon Indians claim in the Yukon and with the rhetoric that often accompanies self-government discussions in the western NWT, both of which put great symbolic store in the concept of First Nations citizenship. Key provisions of the TFN claim address the question of specifying who the beneficiaries are – i.e., Inuit – for purposes of the claim, but this is a very practical issue quite different from the abstract, highly symbolic notion of citizenship.

The ever pragmatic Inuit were not prepared to leave undecided the crucial date for the creation of Nunavut. The agreement that Nunavut would become a reality no later than April 1, 1999 thus met the Inuit demand for a firm date, while allowing sufficient time for proper planning for the new territory. Since the various boards established under the claim, such as the Nunavut Wildlife Management Board and the Nunavut Water Board, would be functional well before division, this date also avoided problems that might have arisen were the two sets of institutions to come into existence simultaneously. The 1999 date was also important from a training perspective. Quite simply, much of the rationale for Nunavut would be undermined if large numbers of experts and bureaucrats had to be brought in from southern Canada to run the new government because of a shortage of trained northerners. The Accord thus notes this human development priority: "the parties recognize the central importance of training in enabling Nunavut residents to access jobs resulting from division...and that investing in people is of greater value than investing in infrastructure" (section 9.1). However, the training and education issues addressed by the Accord in anticipation of the creation of a Nunavut public government in 1999 were separate from the financial support to Inuit for training associated with implementation of the claim.

The phased approach to the transfer of administrative responsibilities to the new government, as set out in Part 6 of the Accord, complements this interest in having as many Inuit as possible ready to assume new government jobs. Part 6 provides for a time frame for full implementation of division that extends beyond the actual date of division in 1999.

At division, a number of key governmental institutions, such as an Assembly and cabinet, will have to be in place, as will personnel, finance and public works functions. Other matters, such as education, health and transportation, even though they will fall under the legislative jurisdiction of Nunavut as of 1999, can "be discharged through intergovernmental agreements or contracts with appropriate governments, public institutions or non-governmental bodies" (section 7.2). An important clarification is necessary here: as of April 1999, the Nunavut Government will have full responsibility for the entire range of jurisdictions currently exercised by the GNWT (plus any transferred to it between now and 1999), but during an initial period it may contract with private sector organizations or with other governments to deliver certain programs and services on its behalf. This is very different from a phased transfer of responsibilities, in which another government (either the GNWT or Canada) would continue to hold jurisdiction.

The Accord called for a Nunavut Implementation Commission (NIC) to oversee division planning for the east. The NIC would be composed of three members nominated by the TFN, three by the GNWT and three representing the federal government, with a Chief Commissioner acceptable to all. The organization and function proposed for the NIC in the Accord were subsequently realized almost verbatim in the Nunavut Act.

Where the costs of division are concerned, Canada agreed to "fund reasonable incremental costs arising from the creation and operation of the Government of Nunavut" (section 8.4). Cost is, of course, a highly important issue, particularly in light of the federal government's goal of deficit reduction through spending cuts. A 1991 study by Coopers and Lybrand projected the once only, start-up costs of Nunavut at more than $500 million and annual incremental costs (that is, additional costs incurred as a result of having two sets of governmental structures) at a minimum of $160 million.[11] When the same firm reviewed these questions, employing a different methodology and set of assumptions, it estimated start-up costs at $340 million and average incremental costs at $50 million annually in the period 1992-2008.[12] More recently, Price Waterhouse put initial costs at about $230 million.[13] Although no consensus has yet emerged even as to the range of costs for establishing and operating the Nunavut Government, the process will clearly be very costly. Moreover, the cost of the Nunavut Government will be entirely separate from the payments to the Inuit under the claim.

The levels of funding from Ottawa for Nunavut are impossible to predict precisely. However, from a comparison of the economic bases of Nunavut and the Western Territory it is clear that Nunavut will, for some time, depend more heavily on federal transfers. The private sector is far larger and more diverse in the west than in Nunavut. The relatively underdeveloped state of the economy of the central and Eastern Arctic will severely limit Nunavut's capacity to generate its own revenue through taxation, and it will thus rely heavily on funding from Ottawa for basic operations.

The boundary plebiscite was not the only critical vote for Nunavut in 1992. Following the signing of the Nunavut Political Accord in October of that year, the TFN claim was put to a ratification vote of all beneficiaries age 16 and over. Just over 80 percent of eligible voters turned out for the November vote, 85 percent of whom indicated their acceptance of the claim, and by extension, of Nunavut.

The debate over division was not limited to people living in the NWT. Saskatchewan and Manitoba Dene expressed concerns and subsequently resorted to legal action to block the creation of Nunavut. They argued that recognition of Nunavut would jeopardize their claims for land overlapping Nunavut that they considered as their traditional territory. Their attempts at intervention were not successful, but they illustrate the range of difficulties faced by the Inuit in finalizing their land claim and the associated division of the NWT.

In consultation with the GNWT and the TFN, Ottawa prepared the Nunavut Act, which was tabled in Parliament in June 1993 along with legislation giving effect to the land claim settlement. For a major bill, with enormously far-reaching implications, the Nunavut Act was passed in an amazingly short time, with only a single day of debate in the Commons and two in the Senate. Its smooth passage reflected the level of popular support it enjoyed. All political parties joined on a non-partisan basis to give their support to the bill. This was particularly notable given the fractious political climate of the day, with the embattled Progressive Conservatives, almost at the end of their mandate, facing an imminent election under their new leader. With these factors influencing the parliamentary environment, the tabling of legislation to institute the largest land claim in history was a matter of particular sensitivity. The Nunavut bill was one of the last passed by Parliament before it was dissolved prior to the 1993 general election.

International interest in Nunavut was considerable. Media around the world carried the story, including such diverse outlets as Russian and Australian television, the *New York Times* and Spain's *El Pais*.

Implementing Nunavut

The Nunavut Act became law in June 1993. The act, which closely follows the direction of the Nunavut Political Accord, sets out the basic framework for the new government and creates processes for managing the transition to division. The October 1993 federal election and the ensuing change of government caused several months' delay in the appointments to crucial boards and commissions, but all of the critical agencies have now been established and have begun their work.[14] The agency most central to the implementation of the Nunavut Government is of course the Nunavut Implementation Commission. Although it maintains an Ottawa office, the Commission headquarters are in Iqaluit. More significantly, all but one of the members of the Commission are Inuit. The non-Inuk speaks Inuktitut and has lived and worked as a teacher and businessman among the Inuit. The NIC is therefore perceived as a body representative of the Inuit interests. On various occasions, commissioners have identified themselves as the "government in waiting" for the new government of Nunavut, and the chairman, John Amagoalik, is commonly referred to as "the father of Nunavut." Consequently, the Commission and its efforts in building the new government will not be perceived as an arm of Ottawa under the direction of central Canadian bureaucrats without the input of the Inuit for whom Nunavut is designed.

The Commission, together with the GNWT and the federal government, have a daunting task before them: creating a new geo-political entity by April 1999. While this might seem to allow sufficient time for transition, considering the mandate, the nature of the task is clearly substantial. Not only must basic questions of organizational design be addressed and extensive training programs mounted, but mundane – yet critical – logistical matters must be settled. Given the difficulties and long lead-times involved in major construction projects in the Eastern Arctic, deadlines are already looming for decisions concerning the extensive infrastructure that will be needed to house the Nunavut government and its employees.

A fundamental principle underlying the implementation of Nunavut is the acceptance that the new government will not be a subordinate or junior territory relative to the Yukon or the NWT. From the outset, it will have the same range of legislative and executive authority as the other territories. At the same time, it is recognized that it may not be possible to prepare the administrative apparatus necessary to manage a full range of territorial programs and services by 1999, especially if the goal of maximum Inuit employment in the new territorial civil service is to be achieved. As discussed below, NIC strongly favours a minimal phase-in period.

This poses some interesting challenges to the implementation process. Canada, the GNWT and the TFN agreed that provision should be made for the possibility of contracting-out delivery, on an interim basis, of many programs for which the Nunavut Government will be responsible. The Nunavut Act authorizes such contracts, and if this approach is taken it is possible that many of these contracted management services will be negotiated with the western territorial government. By taking this approach, Nunavut can be a fully responsible and representative government following the first territorial election since it will be capable of legislating and providing a complete range of services to Nunavut residents. At the same time, the longer transition period that could run well into the new century allows for the realization of the other principles in the Nunavut Political Accord, including maximum hiring of Inuit and provision of services as close to the community as possible.

Two other key provisions of the Nunavut Act are designed to ensure a smooth transition. First, an Interim Commissioner is to be appointed before 1999. This senior administrator will ensure that staff are hired and contracts are in place so that on the very first day Nunavut opens its doors, it can offer a functioning administrative apparatus. Secondly, the Act also stipulates that Nunavut will adopt the body of laws currently in place for the NWT until such time as the Nunavut Legislative Assembly is elected and can pass laws modifying or replacing these NWT statutes. This will prevent a legislative vacuum during the transition period.

A wide range of structural and jurisdictional issues need to be resolved with regard to the relationship between the Nunavut government and the various public government boards established under the TFN claim. Not only must care be taken to avoid overlap and duplication, but mechanisms and approaches to promote cooperation will also be essential.

The Nunavut Act confirms that, whatever other challenges it may face, the NIC does not have to confront very basic issues as to form of government, such as those bedeviling the western NWT. In terms of political decision making, the Nunavut government will, at least at the outset, be essentially a scaled-down, Inuktitut-speaking version of the current GNWT. That is, it will generally follow the modified Westminster model of government that now functions in the NWT, in which a cabinet is chosen by and from elected members of the Assembly.[15] (If, however, the premier is to be directly elected – as many in Nunavut wish[16] – this will imply a substantially different form of government, since direct election of the first minister is incompatible with the Westminster model of cabinet-parliamentary government.)[17]

The act is flexible enough to permit the people of Nunavut to restructure their government quite fundamentally, but for its initial years at least, the Inuit will be content for Nunavut to follow the form of government they already know. One element that will probably be carried over from the present NWT Assembly is the absence of political parties; the all-but-universal presumption is that the Inuit will continue to avoid party politics for some time. Over the longer term, however, the possibility that political parties will emerge should not be entirely discounted. The NIC's December 1994 discussion paper on the Nunavut legislature contemplates this possibility in analysing the size of the Assembly. This paper also proposes an innovative approach to ensuring gender balance in the Nunavut legislature: two-member constituencies in which voters would elect one man and one woman.[18] Response to this proposal from Inuit political leaders has been mixed.[19]

The NIC will not have to resolve basic questions about the nature of community government and its relation to the central territorial government. Although the Nunavut government may well wish to delegate significant powers to communities, this can be accomplished within the existing structure of municipal government. Since the Inuit have no equivalent to the bands or band councils established under the Indian Act, local government in the eastern and central Arctic is entirely public government. Thus, the complications that arise in the west from the coexistence of band councils and municipal governments within individual communities are not present in Nunavut. Tensions and disagreements will doubtless develop between community governments and the Nunavut government but they will probably not be grounded in fundamentally different conceptions of governance, as is the case in the west.

A key issue in the process of establishing a Nunavut territory is the choice of the capital city. The NIC is not responsible for this choice, but rather for recommending a process to the federal government for identifying the best location for the capital. As with most issues in the North, the choice of a capital is no simple matter. Rankin Inlet and Iqaluit are the front runners, but Cambridge Bay also has its supporters. The final choice will doubtless reflect both logistical and political factors. Rankin Inlet is closest to the centre of the territory and can call on formidable political resources, but its weather can be problematic for air travel. Iqaluit's location at the edge of the territory tells against it, but as the largest community in Nunavut and the transportation hub of the Eastern Arctic, Iqaluit has a far more extensive and sophisticated infrastructure than other Nunavut communities. At the same time, and for some of the same reasons, dislike of Iqaluit is widespread in Nunavut.[20]

The political sensitivity of the choice of a capital for Nunavut should not obscure the fundamentally important principle of decentralization in the design of the new government. In addition to a presumption that individual communities will take far greater responsibility for policy development and service delivery than at present, it is expected that territorial administration will be extensively decentralized. Not only will departmental head offices be found in several communities, but administrative subunits will also be distributed throughout Nunavut. The NIC has proposed that headquarters functions be situated in regional offices and auxiliary regional offices in communities throughout Nunavut and that program and administrative authority be extensively devolved to regional and community level staff.[21] Decentralization of this magnitude will reflect both opportunity and necessity. On the one hand, establishing new governmental structures offers the opportunity for sharing the benefits of stable, high-paying jobs throughout Nunavut, and should also give residents a genuine sense of involvement in their government. On the other hand, extensive decentralization can hardly be avoided, since the Nunavut government employees and their families will number well over 1000. Given the size of Nunavut communities, none of them could possibly accommodate more than a relatively small proportion of the new bureaucracy without massive social and physical upheaval.

In designing the new government, the NIC must thus not only take into account administrative and organizational factors, but also geographic and logistical concerns. It must also develop a training plan that will best meet the goal of ensuring that as many Inuit as possible are able to assume jobs within the new government. Indeed, from the outset, developing adequate training programs and facilities has been perhaps the most crucial and problematic task facing the NIC.

An important set of related issues is, however, beyond the NIC's jurisdiction: the division of assets and liabilities between the new western government and Nunavut. There can be little disagreement that the Legislative Assembly Building is a western facility, given its location in Yellowknife, but to what degree, and on what basis, should the financial package for the two territories compensate the east for the fact that this facility is in the west? This is only one instance of a wide range of specific facilities and structures whose disposition will have to be considered in the division of assets. In a few cases, the GNWT has already taken steps to prepare for the organizational consequences of division. Arctic College, for example, is being reconfigured into separate divisions for the

Eastern and Western NWT, the Petroleum Products Division of the Department of Energy, Mines and Petroleum Resources has been split between Fort Simpson and Rankin Inlet in anticipation of division, and the transportation and economic development departments have announced plans for the appointment of assistant deputy ministers with specific responsibility for the Nunavut region.

To assist in implementing division, the GNWT has established a Special Joint Committee of the Legislative Assembly on Division. The committee has equal representation from eastern and western MLAS (including ministers). Its mandate is to ensure that due consideration is given to both eastern and western interests in the division of the territories. Not only must it review, advise on and expedite plans for division of assets, but it must also work on legislative and constitutional issues arising from division. The extent to which this committee will have a bearing on the outcome of division is not yet clear. There is a small division secretariat within the GNWT, which works closely with the Joint Committee, both directly and through a series of working groups that also include representatives from affected groups such as the NIC. Given its explicitly political nature, the Joint Committee is the prime body with broad responsibility for reconciling eastern and western interests. Its success is therefore crucial to the successful implementation of division.

Even more crucial to the success of Nunavut will be effective measures to ensure that sufficient numbers of trained Inuit will be available to run the new government. As noted above, although Nunavut will be a public government, much of the rationale for its existence will be undercut if, for want of trained Inuit, a high proportion of its key bureaucratic positions have to be filled by non-Inuit from southern Canada. Current numbers of Inuit graduating from high school, let alone from college or university, fall well short of what will be needed to fill the host of administrative positions that Nunavut will require. Not all Inuit aspire to be bureaucrats, of course, and even for those interested in and trained for adminstration the Nunavut government is by no means the only option. Such people are much sought after by Inuit organizations, such as the Nunavut Tunngavik Incorporated (NTI) and the regional Inuit associations, as well as by municipal governments and by the private sector. Improvements to the education system and training programs are thus very high priorities for the NIC and for the Nunavut Implementation Training Committee. Despite the substantial efforts made by these and other organizations, however, the availability of trained, educated Inuit to run Nunavut is problematic.

At the political level, while training may not be the issue, the relatively small talent pool for the numerous political offices certainly creates similar problems. Only a small proportion of any population is suited to political life and amenable to its demands, yet Inuit are called upon to fill numerous positions in the legislature, in municipal councils, in the NTI and the regional Inuit associations, and on the boards established under the claim. In the past few years a number of Inuit leaders have fallen victim to alcoholism, violent behaviour or simple burnout from the relentless workloads, the endless travel and the resultant stress of their positions. As in the bureaucratic realm, the limited population base and the large number of elected offices suggests that an adequate supply of Inuit political leaders capable not only of charting political direction for Nunavut but also of enduring the formidable pressures of public life is by no means assured.

In preparing for its first major report, the NIC attempted to be broadly consultative. It held numerous meetings with political leaders throughout Nunavut and the NWT, and organized a large public gathering in Iqaluit in February 1995 at which delegates from all Nunavut communities and Inuit organizations, as well as MLAs and GNWT officials discussed proposals for the governance of Nunavut. The NIC also conducted extensive community tours in late 1994 and early 1995, centred on public community meetings. These meetings gave the Commissioners an opportunity to explain their task (which was often confused in the public mind with the work of the NTI) and to solicit the views of the people of Nunavut as to how their government should operate.

In May 1995, the NIC published *Footprints in New Snow*, its report to the federal and territorial governments and to the NTI setting out its views and recommendations on a host of design issues. The report was premised on a vision of a much leaner central government apparatus than previous studies had presumed. Whereas earlier reports by Coopers and Lybrand had suggested headquarters complements of 1180 and 930 (depending on underlying assumptions), the NIC's scaled-back version proposed only 555.[22] NIC also argued strongly for a much faster phase-in of Nunavut's administrative capacity than had initially been thought desirable (in some quarters, it was assumed this would take the better part of a decade). It proposed that on April 1, 1999, the Nunavut Government be "equipped with fully functioning headquarters operations in relation to virtually all departments and agencies."[23] Arguing that the smaller government it envisaged would make a more rapid phase-in of administrative capacity less problematic, the report emphasized the economic and political importance of Nunavut being able to deliver its own policies as early as possible. Political uncertainty in the Western NWT was also cited as a major reason for accelerating the phase-in; it would be unwise, in the NIC's view, for Nunavut to depend on the unsettled institutional framework of the West for key services.

The NIC report proposed that the government consist of a small number (10) of wide-ranging departments, with extensive decentralization of staff and functions. The report recommended that the three existing administrative regions – Baffin, Keewatin and Kitikmeot – be retained, but that no regional level of government be established between the communities and the territorial government.

On the contentious issue of choosing a capital, NIC put the onus directly on Ottawa. Beyond limiting the choice to Iqaluit, Rankin Inlet and Cambridge Bay, and recommending against a plebiscite, the Commission indicated its willingness to accept the federal government's choice for the capital. (NIC's estimates suggested only marginal capital and operating cost differences among the three contending centres.) The report proposed creation of facilities to allow the Legislative Assembly to hold regular sessions in each region.[24]

Other significant features of the report were its emphasis on the need to capitalize on the possibilities of new communications technologies and its concern about equitable treatment of Nunavut *vis-à-vis* the Mackenzie Valley in the run-up to division.[25]

The report left a number of issues for further consideration – for example, the composition of the legislature and the direct election of the Premier. It did, however, provide sufficiently clear direction and enough detail on administrative design to allow the federal government to develop specific logistical and financial plans to realize its role in creating Nunavut. Indeed, the nature and the timing of the report were explicitly premised on the notion of presenting recommendations to Ottawa so that a cabinet submission leading to funding and detailed implementation decisions could be prepared by fall 1995.

Nunavut and Inuit Self-Government

If the distinctions between the Nunavut Government and the TFN claim provisions can be confusing, they nonetheless underline the important fact that the Inuit have not put all their political eggs in one governmental basket. They are protected by having a Nunavut territorial government that they will control since the territory comprises a substantial majority of the population. The land claim further protects their interests in both Nunavut and their settlement region, through Inuit involvement in the management of resources in those areas.

The claim establishes public government structures with guaranteed Inuit representation to oversee and control critical aspects of economic activity, both traditional and modern, in Nunavut. The Nunavut Wildlife Management Board, created under Article 5, and the Nunavut Planning Commission for land use planning, established under Article 11, are particularly important. In addition, attention to Inuit interests in the review of proposals for major economic development projects is assured through a Nunavut Impact Review Board (Article 12). Similarly, Inuit have substantive representation on the board that manages water, the Nunavut Water Board. Articles 15 and 16 of the claim reflect the importance of Inuit off-shore harvesting practices by authorizing a number of the boards to exercise off-shore jurisdiction.

Significant differences of opinion exist as to the extent to which these public bodies protect Inuit rights to land and their control over resource management and, more generally, as to whether they embody genuine self-government for Inuit. A recent editorial in the *Nunatsiaq News* addresses these issues forthrightly: "Although Inuit are a majority of the population, the land claim sets up public boards with non-Inuit representatives and in some cases with final decisions made by a public government minister. This is not self-government."[26]

Guaranteed Inuit involvement in these public boards is nonetheless highly important for it protects the fundamental relationship between the Inuit and their traditional land and wildlife pursuits. In most cases these are decision-making, not advisory bodies. These institutions are well positioned to protect Inuit interests when matters that may affect traditional lifestyle arise.

A case in point was the ill-considered decision by the federal minister of Fisheries and Oceans in June 1994 to reduce turbot quotas in Davis Strait. The decision was announced without consultation with the Nunavut Wildlife Management Board or any Inuit organization, in direct violation of Article 15 of the claim. Although the Inuit recognized the conservation objectives that lay behind the decision, they took the minister and the department severely to task for ignoring the claim. Backed by the GNWT and the NTI, the organization established through the claim to represent all Inuit in the Nunavut settlement area, representatives of the NWMB elicited an acknowledgement from the minister that he had overlooked the claim in reaching his decision and a commitment to consultation with Inuit on questions affecting fish stocks in waters covered by the claim.[27]

Another significant element in the protection of Inuit interests is the Inuit insistence that their commitment to Nunavut as an expression of their aspirations for self-determination has not extinguished the potential for their pursuit of self-government arrangements at a later date. The Inuit have made it clear that they expect the Nunavut government to meet their self-governing interests for the foreseeable future. Nevertheless, were there to be a significant demographic shift due to a declining Inuit population or to increased migration to Nunavut, the Inuit believe they would be able to approach Canada regarding the recognition of inherent right powers either through Aboriginal institutions, or through new guarantees of Inuit involvement in territorial decision-making bodies.

Given the language of the land claim, which makes no direct reference to extinguishing the self-government interests or rights of the Inuit, Canada would probably accept some form of self-government negotiations under the inherent right umbrella. Should this occur, the federal government would probably expect some reconciliation by the Inuit of their interest and participation in the Nunavut Government and their self-government aspirations. The fiscal pressures faced by Canada would strongly militate against acceptance of a distinct Inuit-specific set of institutions separate from the Nunavut government which, in itself, has been a significant, and potentially costly, concession by Canada.

The extent to which the Nunavut government and the public government boards established under the claim operate to promote and protect Inuit interests will be significantly affected by the NTI. As successor to the TFN, its prime responsibility lies in the implementation and oversight of the claim, though it interprets this mandate in a very broad fashion, for example, by organizing conferences on economic development prospects in Nunavut and developing plans for a hunter support program. Its leadership is elected on a Nunavut-wide basis and can thus claim a broader base of support than that of MLAs. This is not to suggest that the NTI and Inuit MLAs work at cross purposes. Indeed, a noteworthy feature of Nunavut politics is the periodic "summit" meeting of all Nunavut leaders, including the MP and MLAs, NTI leaders, NIC commissioners, representatives of regional associations and others. These meetings are important to ensure unity of purpose and smooth coordination among the various organizations and representatives involved in the creation of Nunavut. They are primarily, though not exclusively, Inuit gatherings; for example, non-Inuit MLAs representing Nunavut constituencies attend as full participants.

As an organization that combines strong grass-roots support with extensive legal prerogatives under the claim, the NTI is a powerful player in Nunavut politics. It will undoubtedly forge a close set of links with the Nunavut government, quite unparalleled in any other Canadian province or territory, although the precise dimensions of that relationship will doubtless take some time to emerge fully.

Conclusion

The relationship between Canada and Nunavut is, in several ways, unique and indeed inherently different from the relationship between the national order of government and the other partners in the federation.

At root, Nunavut represents the outcome of a political agreement between an Aboriginal people and the federal government. Despite the similarities between the Nunavut Act and the NWT Act, fundamental innovations in the former affirm the inseverability of Inuit interests and the new territory thereby setting Nunavut apart from the provinces. Section 25 of the Act delegates to the Nunavut government, albeit in a limited sense, federal legislative authority under section 91(24) of the Constitution Act, 1867 for "Indians and land reserved for Indians":

> For greater certainty, the Legislature may make laws under any other provision of this Act for the purpose of implementing the land claims agreement entered into by Her Majesty in right of Canada and the Inuit on May 25, 1993 or any other land claims agreement with an Aboriginal people as may be designated by order of the Governor in Council.[27]

Thus, through the new territory's "constitution," the Nunavut Act, the Inuit have secured further capacity to control their Aboriginal interests, through a public government body that they control.

Although it does not carry the same significance, another section – 23(1)(n) – also reflects the unique relationship between the Nunavut government and its majority Aboriginal population. This section authorizes the territorial government to legislate for "the preservation, use and promotion

110

of the Inuktitut language..." This is far more than symbolism, since Inuit leaders plan for Inuktitut to become the working language of the Nunavut government. (The realization of this goal will depend heavily on the success of education and training initiatives.)

These provisions underline the distinctive Aboriginal foundation of the new territory. This legal foundation, the inseverability of the Inuit's interests and the new territorial government, and the close linkages that will doubtless emerge between the Nunavut Government and the various public government boards established under the claim, arguably create a constitutional framework for the territory that is quite distinct from that of the provinces. Section 25 in particular gives Nunavut an explicit constitutional role, extracted from the jurisdiction of Canada, that is not enjoyed by the provinces.

This distinction in the constitutional foundations of the provinces and of Nunavut represents an important new linkage between cultures and governments in this country. The creation of Nunavut, in other words, is a powerful and visionary step forward for Canada's Aboriginal people and for Canada itself. The provincial model of government, founded on the British parliamentary structures and traditions, has been modified to give the Aboriginal people of the Nunavut region extensive jurisdiction over their inherent Aboriginal interests.

An important question links the discussion of the emergence and nature of Nunavut in this chapter to the subsequent consideration of national constitutional concerns and the implications of the territories' emerging constitutional presence in the chapter, "The North on the National Stage." The question turns on the Inuit position regarding their inherent right to self-government. If the federal government proposes a definitive statement on the inherent right, as is the intent of its current consultations, will the Inuit wish further constitutional clarification of their inherent right as embodied in the public government of Nunavut? Will the Inuit call upon the federal government to accord Nunavut the same constitutional recognition and protection as may be acquired by other Aboriginal peoples' self-government? If so, Nunavut will take another major step away from the traditional course of political evolution experienced in the provinces and will become all the more closely tied to the Aboriginal parent responsible for its creation.

Thus, aside from a host of practical decisions arising in the implementation process, two issues fundamental to the future of Nunavut remain open. The first follows the outcome of the inherent right debate. The federal government has already accepted the principle of Aboriginal peoples' inherent right to self-government, and its concrete policy expression could result in a fundamental rethinking of claims and self-government obligations throughout Canada. In this case, the status of Nunavut as the expression of Inuit self-government might have to be revisited. The question would then arise as to whether the federal government would accept constitutional entrenchment of a public government under section 35 of the Constitution Act, 1982 and how this might affect the balancing of rights enjoyed by all Canadians.

A second, rather less abstract question involves cost. Quite simply, how much is Canada prepared to pay for the Nunavut government? Even with a modest and frugal approach to the establishment of new governmental institutions and the adaptation of existing ones, Ottawa still faces very substantial costs in creating and maintaining Nunavut. Every jurisdiction in Canada is faced with serious fiscal pressures, and few are willing to respond by increasing revenue through taxation. Accordingly, spending cuts, program reductions and government restructuring through downsizing, privatization, delayering and the like have become the order of the day. In short, not only are governments' obligations to Canadians very much open for discussion, but so too are the costs of the government structures that fulfil those obligations. In such a context, there will be strong pressures on the federal government to reallocate funds earmarked for Nunavut. Accordingly, the federal government's willingness to maintain its financial commitment to underwrite the expensive new structures of government for Nunavut is a critical question.

Nunavut will become reality in 1999. If the broad outlines of the Nunavut government are clear, many important issues remain to be resolved. A good many, such as the choice of the capital, the size and composition of the legislature, and the organizational and physical design of government, call primarily for hard, focused work and judicious weighing of options. Others, most notably those requiring improved training and education for the Inuit will not be so easily resolved. And yet, developing the capacity of the Inuit to run their government will probably prove more significant than formal structures and processes in determining Nunavut's success. Expectations are very high throughout the eastern and central Arctic that the creation of Nunavut will bring dramatic improvement in the manifold social problems plaguing the Inuit. Indeed, political development in Nunavut is not an end in itself; it is a means of overcoming the poverty, alcoholism, unemployment, inadequate housing, family violence and suicide, as well as the loss of culture that are all too prevalent in the central and Eastern Arctic. This will be the true test of the Nunavut government.

Notes

1. Canada, Department of Indian and Northern Affairs communiqué, "Nunavut Political Accord Signed," October 30, 1992.

2. The territory of Nunavut and the Inuit settlement area under the TFN claim are generally coterminous, but two important differences are worth noting. First, a number of uninhabited islands in Hudson Strait and Ungava Bay, which are currently within the NWT (and thus will become part of Nunavut) are excluded from the TFN claim. More significantly perhaps, Nunavut extends only to the ocean's high-water mark, with the federal government maintaining jurisdiction beyond that limit, whereas the claim includes off-shore waters.

3. Canada, *Report of the Advisory Commission on the Development of Government in the Northwest Territories*, Ottawa, 1966, p. 151.

4. Canada, *Report of the Advisory Commission*, p. 147.

5. Inuit Tapirisat of Canada, *Nunavut, A Proposal for the Settlement of Inuit Lands in the Northwest Territories*, Ottawa, 1976, p. 1.

6. Inuit Tapirisat of Canada, *Nunavut*, pp. 14-15.

7. John Merritt, Terry Fenge, Randy Ames and Peter Jull, *Nunavut: Political Choices and Manifest Destiny* (Ottawa: Canadian Arctic Resources Committee, 1989), p. 75.

8. Coincidently, some of the lands in question, owing to disputes over traditional usage, were subsequently found to include some of the most promising areas for diamond mining. Although mineral development questions formed part of the dispute, potential diamond wealth was unrecognized in the 1980s.

9. Canada, *Agreement Between the Inuit of the Nunavut Settlement Area and Her Majesty the Queen in right of Canada*, 1993, p. 23.

10. The Nunavut Political Accord is reprinted in the spring 1993 issue of *Northern Perspectives*, Vol. 21, no. 1, pp. 7-8

11. Coopers and Lybrand/Government of the Northwest Territories, *Financial Impact of Division*, 1991, p. 7.

12. Coopers and Lybrand/Department of Indian Affairs and Northern Development, *An Estimate of Costs – Creating and Operating the Government of Nunavut* (December 1992).

13. Nunavut Implementation Commission, *Footprints in New Snow: A Comprehensive Report from the Nunavut Implementation Commission to the Department of Indian Affairs and Northern Development, Government of the Northwest Territories and Nunavut Tunngavik Incorporated Concerning the Establishment of the Nunavut Government*, (Iqaluit, May 1995), p. A-168.

14. The delays led the Tunngavik to threaten legal action; Nunatsiaq MP Jack Anawak, Parliamentary Secretary to the Minister of Indian and Northern Affairs subsequently took responsibility for the delays. See Clara Kolit and Todd Phillips, "Anawak: Blame Me for Delayed Appointments," *Nunatsiaq News*, September 23, 1994, p. 5.

15. In a June 1994 discussion paper, the NIC specifies British-style responsible government as one of the "broad principles" for the Nunavut Government; see Nunavut Implementation Commission, "Discussion Paper Concerning the Development of Principles to Govern the Design and Operation of the Nunavut Government," June 23, 1994, p. 5.

16. Jim Bell, "Nunavut delegates want elected premier," *Nunatsiaq News* March 3, 1995, p. 5.

17. Graham White, "Consequences of Electing the Government Leader of the Northwest Territories," paper prepared for the Strategic Planning Session of the Northwest Territories Legislative Assembly, Cambridge Bay, NWT, October 1993.

18. Nunavut Implementation Commission, "Two-Member Constituencies and Gender Equality: A 'Made in Nunavut' Solution for an Effective and Representative Legislature," December 6, 1994.

19. Jim Bell, "Amagoalik pleads for sexual equality plan," *Nunatsiaq News*, March 3, 1995, p. 3.

20. Baker Lake and Igloolik made bids to become Nunavut's "executive capital" (the site of the legislature but without departmental head offices). This idea would appear both unrealistic and, given its rejection by the NIC, improbable.

21. Nunavut Implementation Commission, *Footprints in New Snow*, pp. 25-26.

22. Nunavut Implementation Commission, *Footprints in New Snow*, p. 31.

23. Nunavut Implementation Commission, *Footprints in New Snow*, p. 39.

24. Nunavut Implementation Commission, *Footprints in New Snow*, chap. 9.

25. Nunavut Implementation Commission, *Footprints in New Snow*, chap. 7 and 9.

26. "Inuit self-government? Not yet," *Nunatsiaq News*, March 25, 1994, p. 7.

27. See Lisa Gregoire, "Feds Get Lesson on Land Claim," *Nunatsiaq News*, July, 29, 1994, p. 1.

Five

The North on the National Stage

Introduction

In the national context, the future of Canada's northern territories depends heavily on the vision of parliamentarians and government leaders, both national and provincial. Without a consensus within Canada's leadership on the place of the territories in its future, this unfinished constitutional business will not be concluded.

This chapter addresses three questions. The first asks what constitutional status the territories currently enjoy. The second question seeks to determine where recent changes in the territories' constitutional position fit in the evolution of the Canadian federal state. The third question focuses on future constitutional development: what practical changes in the territories' status can and should be achieved in the current political environment?

In brief, we argue that because the Yukon and the NWT have a constitutional presence in Canada, they enjoy a different status from that of the territories that existed early in this century. This presence is a function of the language of the Constitution, a new recognition of the territories by the courts and the close linkages between the public territorial governments and Aboriginal land claims and self-government agreements. Despite this constitutional presence, the territories remain vulnerable to both federal and provincial interests and directions. In short, their unsettled constitutional status deserves to be settled.

In putting the case for explicit constitutional recognition, we note in this chapter that nation building in Canada has not followed a uniform path, but has been marked by political compromise and evolving conceptions of national-subnational relations. This suggests that national constitutional treatment of the territories need not conform with past practices but should incorporate new constitutional models to accommodate the unique social and political environments found in the Yukon, the western NWT and Nunavut.

Many in southern Canada assume that provincehood is a foremost political goal for the territories. For most northerners, however, the prospect of provincehood is not of immediate concern; of far higher priority are political-constitutional measures that would accord them full authority and capacity to govern themselves and to control their own affairs. (Of course, as noted in previous chapters, this means radically different things to different people.) In other words, the territories' aspirations and priorities may well be realized through a process of constitutional evolution quite different from that which occurred in southern Canada.

The Territories' Current Constitutional Presence

Judicial interpretations, the language of the existing Constitution and the implications of the various claims agreements in the North all support the thesis that the constitutional status of the territories, though not on a par with the provinces, is nevertheless distinct from that of legislatively subordinate entities such as municipalities (which many nonetheless claim to be the territories' status under Canada's Constitution). The developments that have bestowed constitutional presence on the territories have all occurred since 1982; prior to that year, we suggest, the territories did lack constitutional status.

According to the traditional view of those in the legal community who have pondered their legal and constitutional status, the territories are simply creatures of federal statute. By extension, Ottawa could, at any time and in any way it saw fit, alter representative and responsible government there or indeed do away with it altogether.[1]

The reasoning behind this view runs as follows. The Yukon, NWT and Nunavut Acts are statutes passed by the Parliament of Canada that give executive authority to the territorial Commissioners. The current exercise of the executive function by elected members of the territorial assemblies occurs on the sufferance of the federal government, and in the Yukon rests in large part on letters of instruction issued by the Minister of Indian Affairs and Northern Development to the Commissioner under the authority of the Yukon Act. Legally, the minister could revoke existing letters and instruct the Commissioner to resume all executive functions.

Moreover, with a simple statutory amendment Ottawa could totally abolish the territories' elected assemblies. As noted in chapter 2, this almost occurred in 1919 in the Yukon. An even more extreme possibility is contemplated in section 42 of the Constitution Act, 1982: erasing the NWT or the Yukon from the map by the extension of existing provinces. This could be accomplished through a formal amendment to the constitution realized through the "seven and 50 rule," which requires agreement of Parliament and the legislatures of two-thirds of the provinces constituting at least 50 percent of the total provincial population.

Of course, such developments are highly improbable from a practical political point of view. Yet the question of the territories' constitutional status involves far more than the remote possibility of their abolition and that of their governments: it concerns the nature of territorial government and the territories' place within the Canadian state.

Were the territories' status within Canada's constitutional framework to be challenged legally, the response might surprise the legal purists. In a 1986 judgement on an issue relating to the application of official bilingualism in the Yukon, Mr. Justice Perry Meyer of the Supreme Court of the Yukon Territory rejected arguments describing the Yukon government as a federal agency. Without providing detail, Justice Meyer employed the term "infant province" to describe the territory's relationship to its federal parent.[2] This hardly gives territorial residents cause to celebrate the attainment of constitutional recognition. One judge's passing comment does not a major constitutional judgment make. However, the decision suggests that the courts may see fit to recognize a distinctive territorial presence as fundamental to Canada's geo-political fabric.

Other evidence points to a judicial perception of the territories as having a unique status among the nation's governing institutions. Section 32(4) of the Rules of the Supreme Court of Canada now expressly confirms the territories' capacity to apply in their own right to intervene in an appeal or reference before the court.

This option was used in a 1992 appeal before the Supreme Court, *New Brunswick Broadcasting Co. v. Nova Scotia (Speaker of the House of Assembly)*.[3] In this case the Yukon and the NWT joined a number of provinces as interveners. What is important for present purposes is not so much the court's judgment as the subject of the case, namely the privileges of Canadian legislatures and their relationship to the Constitution and, specifically, to the Canadian Charter of Rights and Freedoms. The point here can perhaps best be rendered as a question. Why would the Supreme Court establish (and Parliament sanction) rules allowing territorial governments to intervene in cases concerning such issues as the powers and privileges of constitutional governing bodies if it does not recognize the importance of constitutional issues to those territorial governments?

The language of the Constitution further bolsters the argument. Section 30 of the Canadian Charter of Rights and Freedoms provides: "A reference in this Charter to a province or to the legislative assembly or legislature of a province shall be deemed to include a reference to the Yukon Territory and the Northwest Territories, or to the appropriate legislative authority thereof, as the case may be."

As Funston and Meehan explain in their recent constitutional law text,

> Parliament's power to amend or even repeal the territorial constitutions appears at first glance to be unfettered; however, s. 3 of the Charter of Rights and Freedoms guarantees certain democratic rights to Canadian citizens. Section 3 says that every citizen has a right to vote in an election of members of a "legislative assembly."[4]

It thus follows that stripping representative government from either territory would breech this Charter right enjoyed by all Canadians. (Nor could such an action be legitimized through use of the section 33 "notwithstanding" provision, which permits override of some Charter protections, since section 3 is exempted from the application of that provision.)

Another set of arguments that point to the existence of a territorial constitutional presence stems from the important role of the territorial governments in meeting Canada's land claims and treaty obligations to the Aboriginal peoples in the North. In southern Canada the federal government has established a system of reserves to meet these obligations, and either delivers provincial-type programs and services directly to the reserve residents, or funds Aboriginal councils to do so. Across the North, only a handful of reserves exist, encompassing little land and few people. With the exception of the Treaty 8 groups, Aboriginal people in the territories have largely chosen to settle their outstanding claims to land ownership through the land claims process. The relationship between First Nations and government (federal and territorial) does not fall under the

Indian Act as is the case for the reserves in the south, but is described and mandated in detail through the land claims agreements and supporting legislation. As noted in previous chapters, a series of public boards, councils and committees has been or will be created to ensure direct Aboriginal involvement in land and resource management throughout the territories. The crucial Aboriginal rights that have been defined through land claims are tied directly to these public management regimes.

The central role of these claims-mandated institutions of public government in expressing and recognizing Aboriginal rights means that Canada cannot in any fundamental way change the structures of public government in the territories without upsetting the political balances created through the claims. The Aboriginal peoples' involvement in these boards and committees is a fundamental aspect of their relationship with Canada and is also a direct expression of their Aboriginal rights, which are constitutionally protected under section 35 of the Constitution Act, 1982. In honouring these claims-related commitments, the federal government cannot alter or dispense with the current instruments of government unless it replaces them with mechanisms through which the Aboriginal people can enjoy the same expression of their rights. In other words, Parliament could amend the claims legislation to abolish the Nunavut Water Board, but it would be constitutionally required to establish an equivalent agency, with equivalent powers and composition (one aspect of which is participation by nominees of the Nunavut government).

This argument is particularly strong where Nunavut is concerned. Not only will the Nunavut government enjoy constitutional presence because of the claim, but the territory's very existence is also inextricably tied to the settlement of the Inuit land claim. Despite careful drafting of the land claim agreement to ensure that the instruments creating Nunavut did not receive constitutional protection, there is no doubt that the genesis of Nunavut is the land claim itself. Doing away with Nunavut would fundamentally breech the modern day, constitutionally protected treaty entered into by Canada and the Inuit people. Furthermore, the very make-up of the territorial government, and its legislative and executive authorities and processes, are defined through a combination of the claim, the Nunavut Political Accord and the Nunavut Act. Substantive alteration of these could be similarly challenged by the Inuit as a breech of Canada's treaty commitment.

Thanks to the relationship between claims and public government, Parliament's capacity to change unilaterally the form and nature of government administration in the North has been severely restricted. At a minimum, any change threatening representative and responsible government in the territories would require substantive consultation with the Aboriginal groups with whom Canada has treaties.

A limited number of federal statutes have gained special constitutional status due to their importance in our governing framework – for example, the Supreme Court Act and the Indian Act, which reflects a broad and unique federal obligation. The term "proto-constitution" has been used to describe the special nature of these statutes. The importance of territorial governments in meeting Canada's claims and treaty obligations in the North suggests that in some manner the Yukon Act, the NWT Act and the Nunavut Act are similarly proto-constitutional in nature. This implies that any amendment to those statutes requires special treatment by ensuring the full involvement of northern residents.

To summarize the situation: in a number of ways the territories have a special, albeit unwritten, constitutional status within Canada. This conclusion is important not because of any significant likelihood that the federal government might attempt to revoke representative and responsible government in the territories or that it might exercise its full legal authority over them through strict adherence to the nominal forms of the Yukon Act, the NWT Act and the Nunavut Act. Much of Canadian constitutional history is a story of voluntary surrender of *de facto* governing authority by institutions imbued with formal powers to nominally subordinate institutions. The formal powers of the Governor General, the Senate, the provincial lieutenant governors, the federal cabinet (*vis-à-vis* provincial governments) are all significantly constrained, if not all but set aside, by powerful quasi-constitutional conventions that determine how Canadian governments actually operate. Just as no Canadian government could contemplate abolishing the Supreme Court of Canada (which, until 1982, existed solely by virtue of an Act of Parliament), nor exercise its prerogative to disallow provincial legislation, no federal government could do away with the institutions of democratic government in the North.

Nonetheless, the territories remain vulnerable to external actions that could affect their ability to determine their evolution. The territorial constitutions, the Yukon Act, the NWT Act and the Nunavut Act, leave the federal minister responsible for the North with substantial power to modify the relationship between the Commissioner, the executive and the assembly. Although provincial lieutenant governors are, like territorial Commissioners, federal appointees, traditions and conventions have evolved in the provinces to limit severely not only their governmental prerogatives but also the federal government's capacity to direct them to exercise their power to reserve provincial legislation. If similar conventions are clearly developing in the territories, as yet no test – political or legal – has confirmed the inviolability of the current government structure or whether the federal minister is restricted in exercising control over the commissioners.

The territories' special constitutional status is therefore an important issue because it illustrates that formal constitutional recognition, as discussed below, would represent a confirmation and extension of existing authority rather than a fundamentally new direction (such as schemes that occasionally arise to entrench municipalities in the constitution or to grant provincial or quasi-provincial status to the larger cities).

Recent Constitutional Developments Affecting the North

The history of the evolution of Canada's governmental institutions is one of accommodation and compromise. Without such accommodation among quite diverse communities of interest, Canada might not have been created out of the British colonies of the 1800s. Nowhere has compromise been more evident than in the initial creation and subsequent development of federalism. The initial division of powers between the federal and the provincial governments, which overwhelmingly favoured Ottawa, has given way to extensive provincial powers over a wide range of governmental activities. The nature of the evolving relationship between the federal and provincial governments is summed up by Andrew Heard:

> The character of Canadian federalism has been significantly shaped by a web of intergovernmental diplomacy that sees many policies implemented by one level of government only after extensive consultations with, and even the express agreement of, the other...In order to understand something of the manner in which Canadian federalism actually functions, one must appreciate the degree to which political practice has forged an informal transformation of the legal division of jurisdictions between the national and provincial levels of government.[5]

In short, the evolution of Canadian federal-provincial relations clearly demonstrates that debate, compromise and agreement have resulted in a dynamic constitutional arrangement that is more sophisticated and sensitive to social and political realities than the express language of the written constitution.

This dynamic and flexible approach to federalism should be the basis for the treatment accorded the northern territories. Their accommodation into the federation can be developed creatively, recognizing the unique place they hold within Canada's social and political geography. And indeed, significant steps have been taken in this direction over the past few years.

The willingness of the federal government and the provinces to take territorial interests seriously and to acknowledge their claim to political standing in national constitutional processes has increased substantially in a relatively short period. This is apparent from a comparison of the provisions of the Meech Lake and Charlottetown accords that directly affected the territories. Although both ultimately ended up on the constitutional scrap-heap, a brief review of how they treated the territories is instructive.

From a territorial point of view, the Meech Lake Accord was an entirely retrograde step.[6] The accord offered nothing positive for the territories, but it stood to adversely affect them in several ways. It would have made the attainment of provincial status more difficult by requiring provincial unanimity for the admission of new provinces, instead of approval by Parliament and two-thirds of the provinces under the "seven and 50 rule." (Prior to 1982, of course, no provincial approval was required.)[7] The practical consequences of this change may have been limited, but the symbolism rankled. In addition, under the Meech Lake Accord, both Senators and Supreme Court of Canada justices were to be appointed on the recommendation of the provincial governments, no role being specified for territorial governments. While the territories would still be entitled to Senate representation, the possibility of territorial residents becoming Supreme Court Justices was effectively eliminated. Furthermore, the accord extended various powers and rights to the provinces but not to the territories. While some, such as provincial involvement in setting and administering immigration policy, were of limited practical import to the territories, the right to opt out of national shared-cost programs and receive financial compensation was an immediate and major concern to them. Finally, the Meech Lake Accord would have constitutionally entrenched regular first ministers' meetings but with no formal provision for territorial participation.

In contrast, the Charlottetown Accord promised concrete improvements for the territories: a return to the pre-1982 conditions for creating new provinces; a requirement of territorial consent for any extension of provincial boundaries into the territories; a formal role for the territories in the appointment of Supreme Court Justices; and entrenchment of the territorial government leaders' participation in annual first ministers' conferences. The accord would also have entrenched in the Constitution the Aboriginal peoples' inherent right to self-government, which would have had profound effects on land claims and governance structures throughout the territories.

This is not the place to pursue a full explanation as to why the Charlottetown Accord treated the territories so much more favourably than the Meech Lake Accord, although the active participation of territorial and Aboriginal leaders, which marked the Charlottetown but not the Meech process, was doubtless a major factor. Indeed, the inclusion of territorial leaders at federal-provincial conferences is a particularly significant indicator of the more accommodating posture that the provinces and the federal governments have adopted toward the territories. A decade ago, territorial government leaders could count themselves lucky to be invited to make brief statements and to join the "photo-op" at the wrapup of first ministers' meetings. Their extensive participation in the discussions leading to the Charlottetown Accord marked an important turning point; today they are regular, if unquestionably junior, participants at all first ministers' conferences. (Another signal that the territorial leaders have become accepted players in such circles was their presence, along with the Prime Minister and the provincial premiers, on the 1994 "Team Canada" trade mission to China.) No less important, though lower in profile, is the territorial ministers' routine participation in, and hosting of, the myriad gatherings of sectoral ministers (such as finance or education ministers) so central to governance in this country.

Still, it is by no means certain that such involvement would prevent a repeat of episodes such as the Meech Lake Accord in which federal-provincial agreements either overlooked or harmed territorial interests. Formal, explicit recognition of the territories' constitutional presence is necessary.

Unfinished Business: The Territories on the National Constitutional Agenda

The unfinished constitutional business of Canada's northern territories encompasses three broad categories of issues: modernization of the territorial "constitutions" (the territorial acts), devolution of remaining province-like powers to the territories and formal constitutional recognition.

With all provinces today enjoying essentially equivalent constitutional status, it is easy to lose sight of the fact that their entry into Confederation followed quite diverse routes. The four original provinces were self-governing colonies united through an act of the British Parliament. British Columbia and Prince Edward Island joined Confederation through British orders-in-council; both struck unique bargains with the federal government as conditions of their entry. Manitoba, though admitted to Confederation prior to BC or PEI, was established by federal statute. Saskatchewan and Alberta were also created by federal statute from a Canadian territory, and for the first 25 years of their existence were denied jurisdiction over natural resources. Newfoundland, which in 1948 was effectively a British dependency, came into Canada through a unique set of negotiations that accommodated its peculiar interests and priorities. In none of these cases was the approval of any of the existing provinces required, as now stipulated in the Constitution Act, 1982; moreover, several provinces had their borders greatly expanded by what amounted to federal fiat. In short, the ways in which new members have been admitted to the federation have accommodated quite divergent interests and approaches.

With key public government structures stemming from constitutionally recognized agreements with Aboriginal peoples, the nature of the territories' constitutional presence in Canada differs profoundly from that of the territories (today's western provinces) in the 19th and early 20th centuries. Although the politics underlying the creation of Canada's provinces differed from region to region, their authority and power derive from a regional interest in autonomous self-governance in local and regional matters, as ultimately recognized and formally enshrined in the Constitution. But those powers and authority did not originate in the provinces' relationship with their indigenous Aboriginal populations, as is the case to a substantial degree with the Yukon and the NWT.

How then should Canada recognize this emerging new regional dynamic in the North? With the creation of the Nunavut territory and the finalization of major land claims agreements with the Inuvialuit, the Inuit, Dene First Nations (the Gwich'in and Sahtu) and Yukon First Nations, debate on constitutional recognition of the territories has become timely.

Recognition of the emerging new territories can occur in two phases. The first is reasonably straightforward, and to some degree has already been accomplished with passage of the Nunavut Act. This simply entails amendment of the Northwest Territories Act and the Yukon Act to confirm in law the nature of territorial government for the Yukon and for the new western NWT territory.

The second — and clearly more important — phase would involve amending the constitution of Canada to recognize the territories. Such a fundamental step would undoubtedly encounter a host of conceptual and political difficulties. As noted earlier, another set of concerns, related to devolution of power from Ottawa to the territorial governments, also raises issues of constitutional status.

Modernizing the Yukon, Nunavut and Northwest Territories Acts

A number of changes, mostly minor in nature, could be made to the territorial "constitutions," the Northwest Territories Act, the Yukon Act and the Nunavut Act, so that they better reflect the reality of government as it operates in the territories today. Neither the Yukon Act nor the Northwest Territories Act has been significantly revised since the 1950s. Although the Nunavut Act is a new statute and provides the model for most of the changes required to update the other two statutes, it too could benefit from certain changes. Changes to the territorial acts fall into two categories: general updating and governance.

Updating the Yukon Act and the Northwest Territories Act to bring them in line with the Nunavut Act would entail the removal of lengthy sections specifying how intoxicants, mentally disordered persons and neglected children are to be treated. The territorial governments now develop and administer programs in these areas as a result of the legislative capacity vested in them by the Yukon Act (section 17) and the Northwest Territories Act (section 16). Although removing the outdated sections would have little policy significance, it would reflect the maturity of the territorial governments, which now fully occupy these fields.

Possible changes under the rubric of governance range from simply confirming existing practice and terminology to authorizing powers required by modern government. Many such changes would not affect the relationship between Ottawa and the territories.

The language of the acts should be altered so that institutional titles conform with those used in the provinces and found in the Nunavut Act (and indeed employed in territorial legislation): the Territorial Council should be named the Legislative Assembly, and the terms Legislature (the Commissioner and Assembly) and Executive Council should be recognized in law. The Yukon Act and the Northwest Territories Act should also follow the Nunavut Act in allowing for judges of the territorial supreme courts to take over the functions of Commissioner when necessary due to absence or illness. Finally, the Yukon and the NWT, like Nunavut, should have the authority to designate their capitals.

The Yukon Act, Northwest Territories Act and Nunavut Act all contain provisions for the federal minister responsible for the North or the federal cabinet to issue instructions to Commissioners regarding their roles. As noted earlier, these instructions have been useful tools in implementing representative government in the territories. Criticism has been expressed, however, that such instructions can be, and in the past have been, issued in secret. For this reason section 6(2) of the Nunavut Act ensures that instructions are made public by their presentation to the Legislative Assembly. Similar provisions should be incorporated into the other territorial "constitutions."

The Canadian Charter of Rights and Freedoms sets the maximum term of a parliament or a provincial legislature at five years, a provision echoed in the Nunavut Act. The current four-year legislative terms in the Yukon and NWT should be increased accordingly. At the same time, the requirement that the federal cabinet approve the early dissolution of a territorial assembly should be repealed. This limitation on traditional responsible government is particularly problematic in the Yukon where governments have argued that it jeopardizes their ability to determine the timing of elections and increases the risk of losing the element of surprise that provincial governing parties enjoy. In keeping with the provisions of the Nunavut Act, restrictions on the size of the Yukon and NWT assemblies should also be dropped.

Section 11 of the Northwest Territories Act requires the Assembly to hold two sessions every calendar year. This is a hold-over from the days prior to the establishment of the capital in Yellowknife when it was thought desirable to hold at least one session a year in the NWT (the other being the traditional session held in Ottawa). Developments have long since overtaken this provision; it should be repealed.

Where legislative powers are concerned, two changes should be made to the NWT and Yukon acts. First, the territories' legislative authority over the implementation of land claims settlements should be specified. In addition, no pressing reason remains for the legal requirement that territorial governments obtain federal cabinet approval prior to signing agreements with Ottawa in fields where Parliament has authorized federal-provincial agreements. Section 23(1)(t) remedies this matter in the Nunavut Act; similar provisions should be enacted in the other statutes.

Two further changes might usefully be made to all three territorial "constitutions." First, the Nunavut Act carries forward from the Northwest Territories Act provisions setting out educational rights for ratepayers and for Protestant and Roman Catholic minorities. The importance of such denominational considerations to the residents of the three regions is highly uncertain. Consultation with the people might well reveal that these provisions are unnecessary and could be replaced by a simple reference to the territories' capacity to legislate in the field of "education."

The Nunavut Act also mirrors the Yukon Act and the Northwest Territories Act by permitting the federal cabinet to disallow any laws passed by the legislature. It is unclear why this protection is continued since section 23(1) of the act ensures the paramountcy of federal legislation: "Subject to any other Act of Parliament, the Legislature may make laws in relation to the following classes of subjects..." Under the Constitution Act, 1867, the federal government retains a similar capacity to disallow provincial legislation, but it is all but universally agreed that this power has fallen into disuse. This constitutional throwback should therefore be removed from the three territorial acts.

With these changes, the territorial "constitutions" would come of age. They would properly reflect the maturity of territorial governments and be grounded in reality rather than in the fading image of how the territories were governed decades ago. Such modernized constitutions would allow the territories to govern their affairs in a manner consistent with (though not identical to) the way provinces govern themselves. To put it another way, as Steven Smyth has suggested, "having granted many of the North's Aboriginal peoples autonomy regardless of population and economic considerations, the federal government will find it increasingly more difficult not to award such autonomy to the territories."[8]

Many of these suggestions for modernization would be unnecessary if the territories had the same power to amend their constitutions as the provinces. Provinces cannot, of course, use this power to expand their authority *vis-à-vis* Ottawa; nor can they ignore the provisions of the Charter. Within these limits, however, they can determine the form and operation of their governing structures. For example, provinces can choose unicameral or bicameral legislatures, and base their electoral systems on single-member plurality or proportional representation principles. Granting the territories the capacity to amend their own constitutions involves more far-reaching issues of constitutional status than does complete devolution to them of province-like powers.

Completing the Process of Devolution

Another important item of unfinished business in the North relates to control over land and resources. Although the land and resource base is at the heart of both Aboriginal and non-Aboriginal interests, with some exceptions it is not under territorial control. Except for lands owned in fee simple by First Nations as a result of claims settlements, most of the land base in the North rests with and is directly managed by the federal government. This permits Ottawa to take actions such as including as fee simple lands approximately 600 square miles of the Yukon in the land claim settlement reached by the Gwich'in of the western NWT, despite the strong opposition of the Yukon government. Similarly, where resource development is concerned, jurisdiction rests with Canada, as evidenced in the recent diamond rush in the NWT. The environmental assessment panel established in late 1994 to consider potential diamond mines was created by and reports to the federal government and operates under federal environmental legislation. Moreover, under the existing division of powers, the federal rather than the territorial government will decide whether the mines go forward.

Genuine political self-determination requires not just structures of government but economic autonomy. Devolution of jurisdiction over land and resources to the territorial governments will not eliminate their fiscal dependence on Ottawa, but it will substantially add to the territories' capacity to generate revenue through royalty and tax schemes. As discussed earlier (see page 35), the territories may not realize a major financial gain from the transfer, but they will be notably more in control of their economic fate.

Devolution of jurisdiction over lands and resources could be achieved through a straightforward federal-territorial agreement followed by legislation, such as those that implemented the health transfer and the transfer of Northern Canada Power Corporation. However, the transfer of land and resources to the territories would offer an ideal opportunity to take an important step in the territories' constitutional development: creation of a territorial Crown. The lack of a "Crown in right of the territories" has both symbolic and practical consequences. Given the centrality of the Crown in the constitutional underpinnings of Canada and its provinces, the absence of a territorial Crown symbolizes the incomplete nature of government institutions in the territories. On a practical level, the lack of a territorial Crown somewhat impedes the realization of territorial ownership of land and resources in their own Crown right and presents some impediments to the transfer of the attorney-general (prosecutorial) function to the territories.

Creation of a territorial Crown would not confer any additional powers to the territories and certainly would not imply provincial status.[9] It would, however, signify the territories' growing maturity and capacity to govern themselves. A formal constitutional amendment would be required to accomplish this step.

As with so many aspects of northern political development, progress on devolution is subject to a wide range of uncertainties. The territorial governments continue to press for jurisdictional transfer, but Aboriginal groups in the western NWT and the Yukon oppose such action until greater progress on self-government is realized, or unless they are involved in negotiations as full participants. Ottawa is generally receptive to further devolution, but the Minister of Indian and Northern Affairs has appointed a special advisor from outside government to review the whole devolution issue. His report, expected during 1995, may significantly alter the process of program devolution to the northern territories.

Formal Constitutional Recognition

The remarkable course of the territories' political development over the past three decades highlights the very substantial strides that can be made toward political autonomy without formal constitutional recognition. Yet the territories have surely reached the stage where their political advances deserve to be protected, and their peoples' capacity to determine the nature of their governments recognized. This requires national constitutional recognition of the territories.

This unfinished constitutional business warrants serious attention and action. The apparent intractability of the Quebec imbroglio and the failure of the Meech Lake and Charlottetown accords have understandably led to a shying away from constitutional questions, yet the North remains a subject that has captured the national imagination. If it can be viewed separately from the Quebec-dominated debate, the constitutional status of the territories may find favourable treatment on the national agenda. Aside from its value for northerners, such a step has the potential to produce an encouraging constitutional success story.

In 1987 the annual premiers' conference agreed to call a first ministers' meeting to discuss the future of the territories. Although no such meeting took place, an opportunity exists for fulfilling this commitment. Section 49 of the Constitution Act, 1982 requires the Prime Minister to convene a first ministers' conference by April 1997 to review the provisions for amending the constitution. One matter falling under this rubric is the mechanism for extending provincial boundaries into the territories. Obviously, this is of fundamental concern to the territories, which have no role under the present amending formula. The 1997 conference would be an appropriate time to resolve this issue by bringing forward a requirement for territorial approval of provincial boundary extension. Such a requirement was one of the non-controversial matters agreed upon during the discussions leading to the Charlottetown Accord.

This in turn raises the broader topic of constitutionally recognizing the territories. Since the establishment of new provinces falls under the amending provisions, the first ministers could legitimately use the 1997 conference to find a way of giving constitutional recognition to the territorial presence in Canada.

This need not entail creating northern provinces. Indeed, as Gordon Robertson has persuasively argued, the *realpolitik* of Canadian federalism renders changing the political and constitutional balance in Canada by adding new provinces an unlikely prospect. Nor, from a financial standpoint, would it be desirable for the territories.[10]

Northerners tend to be pragmatic people; while the prestige of provincehood would certainly appeal to them, what truly matters is the substance of self-determination. This could be achieved constitutionally in various ways well short of creating new provinces. Robertson, for example, has proposed the creation of "autonomous federal territories," whose constitutions would form schedules to the Constitution Act.[11] Another approach might simply involve a short new section explicitly recognizing the three territories and their right to govern themselves without direction from Ottawa, and guaranteeing them a veto over measures that would reduce their power or their territory.

Granting constitutional status to the territories could, without raising the political red flag of provincehood, involve variations of these approaches. No claim on provincial status would be implied; nor would real or symbolic losses to the provinces result from the creation of a territorial Crown, by an explicit acknowledgement of the territories' capacity to amend their own constitutions or by an enumeration in the Constitution

Act of territorial heads of legislative authority. Such changes would, of course, represent significant diminutions of Ottawa's real and potential power over the territories.

For several reasons, national discussion of the North's constitutional status should start well in advance of the 1997 conference. The people of the western NWT have embarked on a process for developing a constitution for the future western territory, and the Inuit of the central and Eastern Arctic are actively implementing their new constitution, the Nunavut Act. While these processes are already well under way in the North, where interest and debate are strong, integration of the northern and national constitutional agendas would be in everyone's better interests.

However, the North's constitutional status, although it directly affects relatively few people – certainly far fewer than does the Quebec question – is a particularly important aspect of a set of issues that are high on the Canadian political/constitutional agenda: the governance of Aboriginal peoples. It is too early to judge whether the unfolding and prospective governmental developments in the territories can serve as a model for Aboriginal governance elsewhere in Canada. Nonetheless, because the focus of discussions on the North's constitutional status is essentially recognition of Aboriginal interests and rights, in some ways it ranks in importance with the Quebec question.

Another reason underlines the importance of a national focus for this issue. The implementation of Nunavut and the transformation of government in the Yukon are progressing in ways generally acceptable to most residents there. The western NWT, however, is beset by potentially fundamental political divisions that could upset the current constitutional development process. A national debate in Canada on the future of the North would strengthen the hand of the leaders who support this regional constitutional discussion. Knowing that their efforts toward formulating a new western territorial constitution might also achieve formal, substantive recognition in the constitution of Canada could have a powerful and unifying effect on that process.

We in no way deny the difficulty or complexity that formalizing the territorial presence in the Constitution would entail. Finding a consensus among provincial and federal leaders on constitutional matters has proven difficult in the past, and provincial premiers will doubtless bring to the table differing perspectives on this topic. Moreover, extensive consultation and involvement of Aboriginal people will be necessary if the process and outcome are to be legitimate for them.

Moreover, constitutional recognition and self-government capacity – for Aboriginal or non-Aboriginal northerners – will ring hollow without adequate financing. Northern governments continue to depend heavily on Ottawa for their funding and are particularly vulnerable to the fiscal restraint Canadians can expect from the federal government for at least the next few years. Thus, in terms of practical effects on northern governments' ability to provide services and programs to their people, the issue of securing stable, adequate funding arrangements with Ottawa is more pressing than the question of constitutional status.

For all this, the timing is opportune for a national focus on the constitutional future of the North. The territories are a constitutional presence in Canada, although the precise outlines of that presence are as yet undefined. It is time to settle the nature of that presence and give it due recognition within Canada's Constitution.

Notes

1. "[G]iven the status of the Yukon Act as a piece of federal legislation, Parliament may amend that statute as and when it sees fit. This point was most strenuously argued by the constitutional expert, Professor R.I. Cheffins. He stated categorically that due to the statutory supremacy of Ottawa, the Yukon has no more guarantee of legal permanency and survival than a school board or municipal government." H.K. Cameron and G. Gomme, *The Yukon's Constitutional Foundations, Volume 2* (Whitehorse: Northern Directories Limited, 1991), p. 7. (This passage summarizes a personal interview with Professor Cheffins.)

2. *St Jean v. Regina* (unreported) S.C.Y.T., Meyer J., September 26, 1986.

3. [1993] 1 S.C.R. 319.

4. Bernard W. Funston and Eugene Meehan, *Canada's Constitutional Law in a Nutshell* (Scarborough, Ontario: Carswell, 1994), p. 131.

5. Andrew Heard, *Canadian Constitutional Conventions* (Toronto: Oxford University Press, 1991), p. 102.

6. For a discussion of Meech Lake from the territorial perspective, see Gurston Dacks, "The View from Meech Lake: The Constitutional Future of the Governments of the Yukon and Northwest Territories," in Rebecca Aird (ed.), *Running the North: The Getting and Spending of Public Finances by Canada's Territorial Governments* (Ottawa: Canadian Arctic Resources Committee, n.d. [1989?]), pp. 69-110.

7. Constitutional lawyer Bernard Funston has questioned whether the Constitution Act,

1982 does in fact require provincial approval for the creation of new provinces. He argues that section 42(1) requires provincial approval only for amendments to "the Constitution of Canada" pertaining to the establishment of new provinces, thus opening the possibility for provinces to be established outside the formal "Constitution of Canada." Bernard Funston, "Caught in a Seamless Web: The Northern Territories and the Meech Lake Accord," *The Northern Review*, no. 3-4 (Summer-Winter 1989), pp. 69-72. This is a debatable, if intriguing, argument in light of the Charlottetown Accord's explicit proposal for reversion to the pre-1982 provisions for creating new provinces. In any event, even if Parliament could unilaterally create new provinces, they would be second-class provinces constitutionally, for they would lack the authority to take part in constitutional amendments.

8. Steven Smyth, "The Constitutional Context of Aboriginal and Colonial Government in the Yukon Territory," *Polar Record*, Vol. 29, no. 169 (January 1993), p. 125.

9. As Gurston Dacks has pointed out, territorial Crowns existed in both the old North-West Territory and Australia's Northern Territory without conveying provincial (state) status. Dacks, "The View from Meech Lake," p. 92.

10. Gordon Robertson, *Northern Provinces: A Mistaken Goal* (Montreal: Institute for Research on Public Policy, 1985).

11. Robertson, *Northern Provinces*, chap. 4.

Six

Conclusion

Each in its own way, the three northern territories are grappling with some of the most basic issues of governance. What should be the individual's relationship to the state? How is the state defined and the legitimacy of its authority established? How is governmental authority allocated between local communities and wider geographic areas? What political institutions offer the best approximations of the governance principles derived from such questions?

These are very abstract questions, questions debated by political philosophers for centuries. Yet in very practical ways, the three territories are working out answers as they develop concrete arrangements between institutions of public government and of Aboriginal self-government, as they allocate power and jurisdiction between territorial, regional and community governments, and as they design the structures of decision making and administration best suited to their people's needs.

The people of the North do not, of course, have carte blanche to create completely new governments. They are limited by such factors as their continuing dependence on Ottawa for the lion's share of their revenue, their subservient constitutional status and the influence of existing government structures. Still, northerners have the opportunity to devise structures and methods of governance according to their particular needs and aspirations in ways that have never been open to most Canadians.

To say that opportunities exist is not, however, to say that agreement can be reached on how they should be realized. Strikingly different visions of society and approaches to governance exist throughout the North, primarily, though not exclusively, reflecting the division between Aboriginal and non-Aboriginal people. The extent to which compromise and accommodation can be devised between competing political world-views is unclear, as is the willingness of political leaders and the general public to accept such compromises as can be devised.

The experiences of the three jurisdictions diverge substantially for historical, sociological and political reasons. The most obvious sources of the different courses of political and constitutional development are the differing Aboriginal presences in the three jurisdictions. The politics in the territories and the nature of their governments can be largely explained by the fact that Aboriginal people represent over 80 percent of Nunavut residents, about 50 percent in the western NWT and fewer than 25 percent in the Yukon. Yet more is involved than sheer numbers. The substantial variations in the nature of the Aboriginal groups, their cohesion and their approaches to political development also explain a good deal about the three territories. Nunavut is an expression of the pragmatism, persistence and unity of the Inuit; the unsettled political situation of the western NWT reflects geographic, linguistic and philosophic divisions among the Dene and the unique position of the Métis; and in the Yukon the tension between general and particular First Nations interests is evident in its political institutions.

In other words – and this is surely a point that applies even more broadly across Canada – Aboriginal peoples by no means conform to a common mould. In particular, their political priorities and approaches can and do vary a good deal.

Most of the specific developments and issues analyzed in this book are rooted in distinctively northern circumstances and thus do not lend themselves to emulation in southern Canada. To be sure, Canadians would be well served by serious reflection on how the NWT can maintain important strengths of the Westminster cabinet-parliamentary system without, as is uniformly the case in southern legislatures, accepting the suffocating rigidity of party discipline. Similarly, the various initiatives of the Government of the Northwest Territories to devolve program responsibility to the community level stand out as some of the most innovative schemes for community political development anywhere in this country. It is at a more basic level, however, that the northern experience offers broadly applicable lessons to all Canadians.

By way of illustration, the remarkable political-constitutional changes in the northern territories over the past three decades and the continuing debates surrounding their political future bring home a crucial truism often overlooked in the south. Political institutions and constitutional regimes do not exist for their own sake; nor is constitutional development an abstract, self-contained exercise in creating and recreating governmental structure. Political institutions exist to meet people's needs. Constitutional development is a process by which people establish and improve the ways in which they govern themselves. The measure of a set of governmental structures is its effectiveness in bringing society's values and resources to bear on the social and economic problems identified as high priorities.

A corollary of this principle relates to the process of constitutional change. For many years, particularly in the NWT, the people had little say in government and none in large-scale constitutional changes. It is surely no coincidence that the past 30 years have been marked by astonishing political-constitutional strides in all three jurisdictions *and* by widespread public involvement and interest in basic constitutional issues. The Yukon, Nunavut and the western NWT have such small populations that perhaps public participation in constitutional processes as experienced there cannot be repeated on a Canada-wide scale. Again, however, it may be the underlying principles rather than the specific techniques that are important. Particularly crucial is recognition of why it all matters: the link between government structures and people's capacity to improve their social and economic well-being.

Like all Canadians, northerners have found themselves shaped and limited by their political institutions. At the same time, northerners have been willing to experiment with government structures and to question whether institutions developed elsewhere are appropriate for their particular needs and circumstances. To be sure, it is easier to pose such questions and to follow through on the responses in jurisdictions such as the northern territories, where institutions are still in their formative stages, than it is in southern Canada. Yet in a country dominated by political institutions of 19th century design and philosophy, it is highly salutary to have concrete examples of far-reaching institutional change – not so much to follow in their detailed particulars as to cite as affirmation of the possibility and indeed the necessity of change.

On a practical level, the progress registered – and the problems encountered – in the melding of Aboriginal self-government and public government structures certainly bear review throughout Canada; almost every province faces issues similar in nature, if less sweeping in magnitude. The provisions in the self-government agreements emerging from the Council of Yukon Indians claim permitting citizens of individual Yukon First Nations to enjoy the benefits of self-government, not just in that First Nation's settlement area but throughout the territory, will be of obvious interest in southern Canada. Another noteworthy northern innovation is found in the treatment of the Métis people; only in the North have Métis been included with Indians in formal land claims agreements and directly involved with Ottawa in negotiating methods for securing a land base.

As should be evident throughout this book, we do not mean to hold up the three northern territories as paragons of political development that have social and economic problems well in hand. Indeed, problems with government are endemic in the North. Nunavut may prove a spectacular failure, the western NWT may descend into balkanized chaos and the Yukon may find itself as constrained by unimaginative political institutions as any province. Northern governments remain distressingly dependent on increasingly uncertain financial support from Ottawa. And the widespread social ills of the North may prove impervious to any set of constitutional arrangements.

If realism rather than wishful thinking is to guide understanding, such dire possibilities must be acknowledged. Yet, as we believe our analysis demonstrates, innovative and important changes are under way throughout the North, changes that will prove highly successful and substantially enhance government's capacity to improve people's lives. Moreover, the political frameworks emerging in the northern territories hold significant promise of accommodating the very diverse world views, interests and aspirations of Aboriginal and non-Aboriginal northerners.

Writing a book about northern politics in the 1990s is much like buying a personal computer. Inevitably, just as the computer is obsolete before it is taken home and unpacked, writings about northern political development are eclipsed by events before they hit the bookstores. Important new political and constitutional developments are sure to occur in the North within months of the book's publication. At the same time, we hope that this book has set out a framework and context for understanding the transitions under way in northern governance that will make such developments more readily comprehensible both in the North and in the South. We also hope we have successfully conveyed to readers "south of 60" something of the dynamism and the sense that politics really matter, both of which make northern governance so uniquely fascinating.

Selected Bibliography

Abel, Kerry. *Drum Songs: Glimpses of Dene History* (Montreal: McGill-Queen's University Press, 1993).

Abele, Frances. "Canadian Contradictions: Forty Years of Northern Political Development," *Arctic*, Vol. 40, no. 1 (December 1987), pp. 310-20.

Abele, Frances and Mark O. Dickerson. "The 1982 Plebiscite on Division of the Northwest Territories: Regional Government and Federal Policy," *Canadian Public Policy*, Vol. 11, no. 1 (March 1985), pp. 1-15.

Aird, Rebecca. *Running the North: The Getting and Spending of Public Finances by Canada's Territorial Governments* (Ottawa: Canadian Arctic Resources Committee, nd [1989?]).

Alia, Valerie. "Aboriginal Peoples and Campaign Coverage in the North," in Robert A. Milen (ed.), *Aboriginal Peoples and Electoral Reform in Canada* (Toronto: Dundurn Press and Supply and Services Canada, 1991), pp. 105-52.

Alia, Valerie. *Names, Numbers and Northern Policy: Inuit, Project Surname, and the Politics of Identity* (Halifax: Fernwood, 1994).

Asch, Michael. "Dene Self-Determination and the Study of Hunter-Gatherers in the Modern World," in E. Leacock and R.B. Lee (eds.), *Politics and History in Band Societies* (Cambridge: Cambridge University Press, 1982), pp. 347-71.

Asch, Michael. *Home and Native Land: Aboriginal Rights and the Canadian Constitution* (Toronto: Methuen, 1984).

Berger, Thomas. *Northern Frontier, Northern Homeland: Report of the Mackenzie Valley Pipeline Inquiry*, 2 vols. (Ottawa: Supply and Services Canada, 1977).

Billson, Janet Mancini. "Social Change, Social Problems and the Search for Identity: Canada's Northern Native Peoples in Transition," *American Review of Canadian Studies*, Vol. 18, no. 3 (Autumn 1988), pp. 295-316.

Boden, Jurgen and Elke Boden (eds.). *Canada North of Sixty* (Toronto: McClelland and Stewart, 1991).

Bone, Robert M. *The Geography of the Canadian North* (Toronto: Oxford University Press, 1992).

Brody, Hugh. *The People's Land: Eskimos and Whites in the Eastern Arctic* (London: Harmondsmith, 1975).

Brody, Hugh. *Living Arctic: Hunters of the Canadian North* (Vancouver: Douglas and McIntyre, 1987).

Cameron, Kirk. "Let the Yukon Evolve," *Policy Options*, Vol. 7, no. 3 (March 1986), pp. 15-19.

Cameron, Kirk. "The True North Strong and Different," *Policy Options*, Vol. 10, no. 9 (November 1989), pp. 33-34.

Cameron, Kirk and Graham Gomme. *The Yukon's Constitutional Foundations, Vol. 2, A Compendium of Documents Relating to the Constitutional Development of the Yukon Territory* (Whitehorse: Northern Directories Ltd., 1991).

Canada. Royal Commission on Aboriginal Peoples. *The High Arctic Relocation: A Report on the 1953-1955 Relocation* (Ottawa: Supply and Services Canada, 1994).

Canadian Arctic Resources Committee. *Changing Times, Challenging Agendas: Economic and Political Issues in Canada's North* (Ottawa: Canadian Arctic Resources Committee, 1988).

Carrothers, A.W.R. *Commission on the Development of Government in the Northwest Territories* (Ottawa: Indian Affairs and Northern Development, 1966).

Clancy, Peter. "Political Autonomy in the North: Recent Developments," in Douglas Brown and Robert Young (eds.), *Canada: The State of the Federation 1992* (Kingston: Queen's University Institute for Intergovernmental Relations, 1992), pp. 225-44.

Clancy, Peter. "Native People and Politics in the Northwest Territories," in Alain-G. Gagnon and James Bickerton (eds.), *Canadian Politics: An Introduction to the Discipline* (Peterborough: Broadview Press, 1990), pp. 559-79.

Clancy, Peter. "Northwest Territories: Class Politics on the Northern Frontier," in Keith Brownsey and Michael Howlett (eds.), *The Provincial State: Politics in Canada's Provinces and Territories* (Mississauga: Copp Clark, 1992), pp. 297-319.

Coates, Kenneth. *Best Left as Indians: Native-White Relations in the Yukon Territory 1840-1973* (Montreal: McGill-Queen's University Press, 1991).

Coates, Kenneth and W.R. Morrison. *Land of the Midnight Sun: A History of the Yukon Territory* (Edmonton: Hurtig, 1988).

Coates, Kenneth and W.R. Morrison. "Yukon: So Far From Power," in Keith Brownsey and Michael Howlett (eds.), *The Provincial State: Politics in Canada's Provinces and Territories* (Mississauga: Copp Clark, 1992), pp. 323-51.

Coates, Kenneth and Judith Powell. *The Modern North: People, Politics and the Rejection of Colonialism* (Toronto: James Lorimer, 1989).

Crowe, Keith. "Claims on the Land," *Northern Perspectives*, Part 1 (November-December 1990), pp. 14-23; Part 2 (January-February 1991), pp. 30-35.

Crowe, Keith. *A History of the Original Peoples of Northern Canada*, rev. ed. (Montreal: McGill-Queen's University Press, 1991).

Dacks, Gurston. "Politics on the Last Frontier: Consociationalism in the Northwest Territories," *Canadian Journal of Political Science*, Vol. 19, no. 2 (June 1966), pp. 345-61.

Dacks, Gurston. *A Choice of Futures: Politics in the Canadian North* (Toronto: Methuen, 1981).

Dacks, Gurston. "The Case Against Dividing the Northwest Territories," *Canadian Public Policy*, Vol. 12, no. 1 (March 1986), pp. 202-13.

Dacks, Gurston. "Political Representation in the Northwest Territories," in J. Paul Johnson and Harvey Pasis (eds.), *Representation and Electoral Systems: Canadian Perspectives* (Scarborough: Prentice-Hall, 1990), pp. 137-54.

Dacks, Gurston (ed). *Devolution and Constitutional Development in the Canadian North* (Ottawa: Carleton University Press, 1990).

Dacks, Gurston and Kenneth Coates (eds.). *Northern Communities; The Prospects for Empowerment* (Edmonton: Boreal Institute, 1988).

Devine, Marina. "The New Western Territory: Balkanization or Federation?", *Northern Perspectives*, Vol. 21, no. 1 (Spring 1993), pp. 10-14.

Dickerson, Mark O. *Whose North? Political Change, Political Development and Self-Government in the Northwest Territories* (Vancouver: University of British Columbia Press, 1992).

Drury, C.M. *Constitutional Development in the Northwest Territories* (Ottawa: Supply and Services Canada, 1980).

Duffy, R. Quinn. *The Road to Nunavut: The Progress of the Eastern Arctic Inuit Since the Second World War* (Montreal: McGill-Queen's University Press, 1988).

Frideres, J.S. and W.J. Reeves. "Political Development and the Plebiscite," *Inuit Studies*, Vol. 11, no. 1 (1987), pp. 107-13.

Fumoleau, Rene. *As Long as This Land Shall Last* (Toronto: McClelland and Stewart, 1967).

Funston, Bernard. "Caught in a Seamless Web: The Northern Territories and the Meech Lake Accord," *The Northern Review*, nos. 3-4 (Summer-Winter 1989), pp. 54-84.

Gardner, Peter. "Aboriginal Community Incomes and Migration in the NWT: Policy Issues and Alternatives," *Canadian Public Policy*, Vol. 20, no. 3 (September 1994), pp. 297-317.

Grant, Shelagh. *Sovereignty or Security? Government Policy in the Canadian North, 1936-1950* (Vancouver: University of British Columbia Press, 1989).

Gray, Kevin R. "The Nunavut Land Claims Agreement and the Future of the Eastern Arctic: The Uncharted Path to Effective Self-Government," *University of Toronto Faculty of Law Review*, Vol. 52, no. 3 (Spring 1994), pp. 300-44.

Hamilton, John David. *Arctic Revolution: Social Change in the Northwest Territories 1935-1994* (Toronto: Dundurn Press, 1994).

Irwin, Colin. "Lords of the Arctic: Wards of the State," *Northern Perspectives*, Vol. 17, no. 1 (January-March 1989), pp. 2-20.

Jull, Peter. "Lights for the North," *Policy Options*, Vol. 6, no. 3 (April 1985), pp. 28-29.

Jull, Peter. "Dividing the North," *Policy Options*, Vol. 6, no. 4 (May 1985), pp. 10-13.

Jull, Peter. "Take the North Seriously," *Policy Options*, Vol. 7, no. 7 (September 1986), pp. 7-11.

Jull, Peter. "Building Nunavut: A Story of Inuit Self-Government," *The Northern Review*, no. 1 (Summer 1988), pp. 59-71.

Jull, Peter. "Redefining Aboriginal-White Relations: Canada's Inuit," *International Journal of Canadian Studies*, Vol. 3, no. 1 (Spring 1991), pp. 11-25.

Jull, Peter. "The Future and the Frontier," *Policy Options*, Vol. 13, no. 9 (November 1992), pp. 25-27.

Jull, Peter and Sally Roberts (eds.). *The Challenge of Northern Regions* (Darwin, Australia: Australian National University, Northern Research Unit, 1991).

Kenney, Gerard. *Arctic Smoke and Mirrors* (Prescott, Ontario: Voyager Press, 1994).

Lewis, Brian. "Choosing a Premier – Responsible to the Northwest Territories House or Its People?", *The Parliamentarian*, Vol. 75, no. 3 (July 1994), pp. C-16-C-18.

MacLachlan, Letha. "Co-Management of Wildlife in Northern Aboriginal Comprehensive Land Claims Agreements," *Northern Perspectives*, Vol. 22, nos. 2-3 (Summer-Fall 1994), pp. 21-27.

Merritt, John. "Nunavut: Preparing for Self-Government," *Northern Perspectives*, Vol. 21, no. 1 (Spring 1993), pp. 3-6.

Merritt, John, Terry Fenge, Randy Ames and Peter Jull. *Nunavut: Political Choice and Manifest Destiny* (Ottawa: Canadian Arctic Resources Committee, 1989).

Michael, Janet Moodie. *From Sisson to Meyer: The Administrative Development of the Yukon Government, 1948-1979* (Whitehorse: Yukon Department of Education, 1987).

Michael, Patrick. "Yukon: Parliamentary Tradition in a Small Legislature," in Gary Levy and Graham White (eds.), *Provincial and Territorial Legislatures in Canada* (Toronto: University of Toronto Press, 1989), pp. 189-206.

O'Keefe, Kevin. "Northwest Territories: Accommodating the Future," in Gary Levy and Graham White (eds.), *Provincial and Territorial Legislatures in Canada* (Toronto: University of Toronto Press, 1989), pp. 207-20.

Purich, Donald. *The Inuit and Their Land: The Story of Nunavut* (Toronto: Lorimer, 1992).

Robertson, Gordon. *Northern Provinces: A Mistaken Goal* (Montreal: Institute for Research on Public Policy, 1985).

Salisbury, R.F. "The Case for Dividing the Northwest Territories: A Comment," *Canadian Public Policy*, Vol. 12, no. 3 (September 1986), pp. 513-17.

Smyth, Steven. "Ministerial Directives and Constitutional Development in the Yukon Territory," *Polar Record*, Vol. 26, no. 156 (January 1990), pp. 7-12.

Smyth, Steven. "The Constitutional Status of the Yukon Territory," *Polar Record*, Vol. 26, no. 159 (October 1990), pp. 289-92.

Smyth, Steven. *The Yukon's Constitutional Foundations*, Vol. 1, *The Yukon Chronology* (Whitehorse: Northern Directories Ltd., 1991).

Smyth, Steven. "The Quest for Provincial Status in Yukon Territory," *Polar Record*, Vol. 28, no. 164 (January 1992), pp. 33-36.

Smyth, Steven. "The Constitutional Context of Aboriginal and Colonial Government in the Yukon Territory," *Polar Record*, Vol. 29, no. 169 (January 1993), pp. 121-26.

Stabler, Jack and Eric C. Howe. "Native Participation in Northern Development: The Impending Crisis in the NWT," *Canadian Public Policy*, Vol. 16, no. 3 (September 1990), pp. 262-83.

Tester, Frank James and Peter Kulchyski. *Tammarniit (Mistakes): Inuit Relocation in the Eastern Arctic 1939-1963* (Vancouver: University of British Columbia Press, 1994).

Usher, Peter. "Northern Development, Impact Assessment and Social Change," in Noel Dyck and James B. Waldrum (eds.), *Anthropology, Public Policy and Native Peoples in Canada* (Montreal: McGill-Queen's University Press. 1993), pp. 98-130.

Watkins, Mel (ed.). *Dene Nation: The Colony Within* (Toronto: University of Toronto Press, 1977).

Weick, Ed. "Can Canada Afford the North?", *Policy Options*, Vol. 15, no. 3 (March 1994), pp. 16-18.

Wenzel, George. *Animal Rights, Human Rights: Ecology, Economy and Ideology in the Canadian Arctic* (Toronto: University of Toronto Press, 1991).

Western Northwest Territories Constitutional Development Steering Committee. *Member Group Research Reports* (Yellowknife: Constitutional Development Steering Committee, 1994).

White, Graham. "Westminster in the Arctic: The Adaptation of British Parliamentarism in the Northwest Territories," *Canadian Journal of Political Science*, Vol. 24, no. 3 (September 1991), pp. 499-523.

White, Graham. "Structure and Culture in a Non-Partisan Westminster Parliament: Canada's Northwest Territories," *Australian Journal of Political Science*, Vol. 28, no. 2 (July 1993), pp. 322-39.

White, Graham. "Northern Distinctiveness, Representation by Population and the Charter: The Politics of Redistribution in the Northwest Territories," *Journal of Canadian Studies*, Vol. 28, no. 3 (Fall 1993), pp. 7-28.

Whittington, Michael S. (ed.). *The North* (Toronto: University of Toronto Press, 1985).

Whittington, Michael S. "Aboriginal Self-Government," in Michael S. Whittington and Glen Williams (eds.), *Canadian Politics in the 1990s*, 4th ed. (Toronto: Nelson Canada, 1995) pp. 3-18.

Wonders, William. "The Changing Role and Significance of Native Peoples in Canada's Northwest Territories," *Polar Record*, Vol. 23, no. 147 (September 1987), pp. 661-71.

Wonders, William. "Overlapping Native Land Claims in the Northwest Territories," *American Review of Canadian Studies*, Vol. 18, no. 3 (Autumn 1988), pp. 359-68.

Zaslow, Morris. *The Opening of the Canadian North* (Toronto: McClelland and Stewart, 1971).

Zaslow, Morris. *The Northward Expansion of Canada, 1914-1967* (Toronto: McClelland and Stewart, 1988).

Zoe, Henry. "Scrutiny of Expenditures in the NWT Legislative Assembly," *Canadian Parliamentary Review*, Vol. 17, no. 4 (Winter 1994-95), pp. 4-5.

Notes on Authors

Kirk Cameron was born in Whitehorse, Yukon and spent his youth and much of his working life in Northern Canada. He has worked in the Executive Council Office and the departments of Education and Economic Development of the Yukon government. After a brief period with the Province of British Columbia, he moved to Ottawa where, since 1991, he has worked in the Department of Indian Affairs and Northern Development; he is currently a director in the department's Northern Affairs Program. He is co-author of *The Yukon's Constitutional Foundations* and has published articles on government in Canada's North.

Graham White is Professor of Political Science at Erindale College, University of Toronto. His teaching and research interests focus on structures and processes of Canadian government, particularly in the provinces and territories. Among his books are *The Ontario Legislature: A Political Analysis, Provincial and Territorial Legislatures in Canada* and several editions of *Politics: Canada* (co-edited with Paul W. Fox). He has published a number of journal articles and book chapters on politics in the Northwest Territories, and has done contract research for the Royal Commission on Aboriginal Peoples.

Recent IRPP Publications

Governance

G. Bruce Doern, *The Road to Better Public Services: Progress and Constraints in Five Canadian Federal Agencies*

Donald G. Lenihan, Gordon Robertson, Roger Tassé, *Canada: Reclaiming the Middle Ground*

F. Leslie Seidle (ed.), *Seeking a New Canadian Partnership: Asymmetrical and Confederal Options*

F. Leslie Seidle (ed.), *Equity and Community: The Charter, Interest Advocacy and Representation*

F. Leslie Seidle (ed.), *Rethinking Government: Reform or Reinvention?*

Social Policy

Adil Sayeed (ed.), *Workfare: Does it Work? Is it Fair?*

Monique Jérôme-Forget, Joseph White, Joshua M. Weiner (eds.), *Health Care Reform Through Internal Markets: Experience and Proposals*

Ross Finnie, *Child Support: The Guideline Options*

Elisabeth B. Reynolds (ed.), *Income Security: Changing Needs, Changing Means*

Jean-Michel Cousineau, *La Pauvreté et l'État: Pour un nouveau partage des compétences en matière de sécurité sociale*

City-Regions

Andrew Sancton, *Governing Canada's City-Regions: Adapting Form to Function*

William Coffey, *The Evolution of Canada's Metropolitan Economies*

Education

Bruce Wilkinson, *Educational Choice: Necessary But Not Sufficient*

Peter Coleman, *Learning About Schools: What Parents Need to Know and How They Can Find Out*

Edwin G. West, *Ending the Squeeze on Universities*

Public Finance

Paul A.R. Hobson and France St-Hilaire, *Toward Sustainable Federalism: Reforming Federal-Provincial Fiscal Arrangements*

Telecommunications

Charles Sirois, Claude E. Forget, *The Medium and the Muse: Culture, Telecommunications and the Information Highway*

Charles Sirois, Claude E. Forget, *Le Médium et les Muses : la culture, les télécommunications et l'autoroute de l'information*

Choices/Choix

Social Security Reform:
IRPP prend position / The IRPP Position
Commentaries on the Axworthy Green Paper

Public Finance:
Répartition régionale des dépenses fiscales touchant les corporations
À qui profitent les avantages fiscaux ?

Health:
Les marchés internes dans le contexte canadien

Série Québec-Canada:
Un Québec souverain et l'union économique Québec-Canada
L'évolution du fédéralisme canadien
La monnaie d'un Québec souverain

These and other publications are available from
Renouf Publishing, 1294 Algoma Road, Ottawa, Ontario K1B 3W8
Tel.: (613) 741-4333 Fax.: (613) 741-5439